MINORITY REPORT

Jack White

MINORITY REPORT

The Protestant Community in the Irish Republic

Gill and Macmillan

First published in 1975

Gill and Macmillan Ltd
15/17 Eden Quay
Dublin 1

and internationally through
association with the
Macmillan Publishers Group

7171 0766 3

Printed in Great Britain by
Bristol Typesetting Co. Ltd
Barton Manor, St Philips
Bristol

Contents

The mere geographical accident of my birth, for which I deserve no credit whatsoever—this fact that I am an Irishman—has always filled me with a wild and inextinguishible pride. I am also proud of being a Protestant, though Protestantism is to me a great historic movement of Reformation, Aspiration and Self-Assertion against spiritual tyrannies rather than that organisation of false gentility which so often takes its name in Ireland. I cannot describe what I feel when English Unionists are kind enough to say, 'Oh, you are in danger of being persecuted by your Roman Catholic fellow-countrymen. England will protect you.' I would rather be burnt at the stake by Irish Catholics than protected by Englishmen.

GEORGE BERNARD SHAW (1912)

Introduction

'A Little Outside of Things'

I F you want to see the Irish Sweeps Derby, the richest of Irish horseraces, you will go to the Curragh on a Saturday in June. If you want to see fifteen Irishmen playing fifteen Welshmen at rugby you will go to Lansdowne Road on a Saturday in March. If you want to see the two top counties battling for the national championship in hurling or Gaelic football, you will go to Croke Park—on a Sunday.

The sporting calendar reflects the pattern of social life; and social life in Ireland is built upon the geological strata of religion. Horseracing was the sport of the landed gentry, who were predominantly Protestants; rugby football was English and upper-class, played in Protestant schools and clubs. Both sports therefore applied the Protestant code of Sunday observance. Gaelic football and hurling, on the other hand, were the sports of the rural Irish, overwhelmingly Roman Catholic, who did not share the Protestant view of the sanctity of the Lord's Day. Their day for sport and pastimes was Sunday.

The dividing lines have become blurred by time and social change. Nobody now supposes horses or rugby to be exclusively the amusement of Protestants. The Royal Dublin Society has added a Sunday jumping competition to its horse show programme, and the sky has not fallen on Ballsbridge. But the observances remain, bearing witness to their roots in the confessional structure of Irish society. 'Religious differences in Ireland are natural facts,' said a writer in the year 1908, 'and all properly constituted Irishmen are intensely interested in them.'[1] And an Irish-American wrote about twenty years earlier: 'If you wish to buy a mackerel from a fish dealer, you always inquire of somebody beforehand the name of his church, and you judge of the quality of the fish, not by the fish itself, but by the theology of the man who sold it.'[2]

* * *

In the 1890s a Protestant in Ireland knew himself to belong to a minority of about one in four. In the Irish Free State, which became the Republic of Ireland, those Protestants who remained found themselves reduced to about one in twenty. With numbers that had become insignificant, with a difference of tradition which they could define only in terms of an outworn political allegiance, they began to feel and to show a lack of confidence in their own identity. 'An Irish Protestant!' exclaims a young man in a novel by Lennox Robinson. 'The words somehow don't blend, do they? I think one will always be a little outside of things.'[3]

They had been a privileged minority; they were left a minority without privilege. It was too early then to see that what had taken place was the overthrow of a landowning ascendancy which happened, for historical reasons, to profess the Protestant religion; the first three decades of the twentieth century marked a stage in the development of Irish democracy, in which most of the Protestants left could be numbered with the *demos*. They had fought for the interests of the Ascendancy, under the banner of the Reformation. When this band of Christian soldiers was scattered, most of the officers had been lost; those who remained were, by and large, the corporals and the foot-soldiers. Lacking leaders, they were at a loss : under what banner were they to regroup? The Southern Protestant could not make common cause with the Northern loyalist : they had parted sympathy years before, and partition had severed them finally. He had some difficulty in feeling himself at one with a new Ireland which— as he was reminded, politely but insistently—saw itself as a Catholic country. He could hardly be blamed if he felt 'a little outside of things'.

* * *

In 1937 Dr Douglas Hyde, the founding father of the Gaelic revival and the son of a Church of Ireland rector, was chosen unanimously as first President of Ireland under Mr de Valera's new constitution. In 1973 Mr Erskine Childers, son of a republican father, and a minister in successive Fianna Fáil governments and a member of the Church of Ireland, was elected as fourth

President of the Republic. His opponent was, as it happens, a Catholic, but religion was never even a shadow of an issue in the campaign.

Between the two events there lies a great change in the climate of popular opinion. The constitution under which President Hyde took office had embodied an article which, while it provided full guarantees of religious liberty, recognised explicitly the 'special position' of the Roman Catholic Church. In 1972 the people voted by referendum, with scarcely a dissenting voice, to delete this portion of the article. Increasingly individuals have been crossing the barriers between institutions. The ecumenical movement has brought both clergy and laymen closer together, and in 1973 the Roman Catholic hierarchy held its first official meeting with the heads of the principal Protestant churches in the pious precincts of Maynooth College. Catholics now attend services in Protestant churches (though they are still debarred from taking holy communion). The Protestant who enters a Catholic church hears mass in English and 'The Lord's My Shepherd', and scarcely feels a stranger. All these changes have been readily absorbed by a people believed to be conservative. The drawing together was vividly illustrated at the end of 1974, when President Childers died suddenly after little more than a year in office. At the funeral service, broadcast by television from St Patrick's Cathedral, the Roman Catholic Archbishop of Dublin and two of his colleagues of the hierarchy were among the congregation.

The new spirit springs primarily, on the Catholic side, from the inspiration of Pope John and the Second Vatican Council; but it must be said that the seed could never have sprouted so freely if it had not fallen on a soil well prepared—on a people already full of goodwill towards their Protestant fellow-citizens. The sickening sectarian strife in the North, far from straining this goodwill, appears to have had the opposite effect. The North has shown that tribalism can lead to barbarism; and in doing so it has given Catholic Ireland a new awareness of the other tribe. There has been a growth of interest, a growth of curiosity, a new desire to explore and understand the traditions of the Irish Protestant as one strand in the fabric of the nation.

But there is no point in reaching out to embrace a fictitious fellow-countryman. It is fashionable nowadays to call on the memory of Wolfe Tone, the patron saint of Irish republicanism, to prove that a Protestant may be as good an Irishman as anybody else. But it is useless to pretend that Irish Protestants as a group ever shared the republican philosophy. By now two generations of them have grown up in an independent Irish state, and there must be few who feel any prior loyalty. But they are entitled to the dignity of their own traditions. Political orthodoxy is too high a price to pay for religious diversity.

*   *   *

I was born a Protestant in Ireland, a member of a minority within a minority : we were Congregationalists in Cork. Our church numbered about fifteen or twenty people in all. We met each Sunday at the YMCA, in an upper room with shiny brown linoleum on the floor, a small organ in the corner, and over the fireplace a stern engraving of an early Christian maiden choosing the lions rather than Diana. My father managed the finances, led the singing, and took a turn in the pulpit when we were short of a regular minister. On Sunday afternoons, however, he liked to go to a football match. This was a matter of private judgment, and private judgment was the core of his belief.

When the church closed for the summer holidays my parents joined the Presbyterians, but we children liked to go to the Methodists : there were more young people, and the singing was always good. I passed the cathedral of St Fin Barre each morning as I walked to school, and thought it the grandest building in the world. (I still find it rather splendid, though I know now that one is supposed to be whimsical about Victorian Gothic.) But it never occurred to me to go inside. It belonged to the Church of Ireland, an institution which had bishops and read prayers out of a book : Protestant, of course, but a little mysterious, and not quite sound.

We knew some Catholics, but we never really mixed with them. My father's firm recruited from each side in turn, as a matter of policy. Many of his clients were Catholics, and it amused him that they sometimes preferred to confide their business affairs to him than to 'one of their own'. In our modest terrace nearly all the neighbours were Catholics, and we were on perfectly amicable terms with them, but there was no intimacy. Once a year, at Christmas, my father went in next door to take a ceremonial drink with old Mr Kirby. That was the extent of our social contact.

Society was, in fact, so organised that, apart from business contacts, Catholic lives and Protestant lives ran on different tracks. Of course we had a maid, and of course she was a Catholic. We thought of her religious life simply as a series of mandatory observances—mass on Sunday, fish on Friday. Occasionally we might be daring enough to peer in through the window of a Catholic church; the size, the darkness, the images, the flickering candles, all filled us with a sense of superstitious dread, and we carried away in our nostrils a curious smell compounded of poor people and incense. The holy picture in a neighbour's house, with the little red lamp always burning before it; the colourful shrines and decorations that appeared in the streets for Corpus Christi; the little girls in their tiny bridal gowns going to make their first communion: all these, the externals of belief, were so remote from our own austere practice that they seemed like the rituals of some foreign tribe.

On the other hand the Protestant tribe, with all its subdivisions, seemed to enjoy a reassuring range of common ground. At boarding school, not far from Cork, all the boys marched out together to attend Morning Prayer in the parish church. At first a formal liturgy seemed awkward and unfamiliar; but basically there was nothing in the forms of the Church of Ireland that could cause unease to a young Nonconformist. We had all been raised on the Authorised Version, and we all sang more or less the same hymns. We were all used to being addressed in the language of evangelism—as labourers in the vineyard, or as brands plucked from the burning. We had heard it from clergymen, from missionaries, from Sunday-school teachers: it was the *lingua franca* of moral uplift. Between us all, Anglican and Dissenter, the divisions were, I imagine, much narrower than those which divided Church from Chapel in England.

It would not have entered our heads, I think, to regard religion as a question of personal belief. Lennox Robinson's young man remarks wistfully: 'I sometimes wish I were a Catholic.' There is no question in his mind that one might *become* a Catholic. This is a matter decided at birth—a matter of inheritance, a matter of upbringing: it is nothing at all so simple as a question of where one goes to church. What we had inherited, in fact, was a religious culture : a complex of customs, traditions, sentiments, loyalties, which I think I can comprehend only in the word *tribe.*

It is a basic convention of the tribal society that nobody ever changes his religion as a matter of conviction. If a change is made it is always for discreditable reasons. It is not unfair, I think, to say that Protestants see a lapse more in its social context, while Catholics tend to see it in religious terms. To Protestants, a conversion to the Catholic Church is a social lapse, a weakening of the tribe, a desertion from the post of duty. To Catholics, a conversion to the Protestant side is a wilful rejection of the one true faith, a kind of spiritual suicide. George A. Birmingham notes that a convert is generally regarded by both sides—not only the side he leaves but the side he joins—as 'a thoroughly untrustworthy person' :

> We prefer men who are true to type. We recognise without resentment the existence of various types and we are on the whole fairly tolerant. In Ireland a man may be a Protestant or a Catholic, a Nationalist or a Unionist, without suffering any serious resentment. He may choose his fold, but he must be a sheep.[4]

Intelligent commentators have agreed with his conclusion : 'We have attained a degree of religious stability which would be simply impossible in a people deeply interested in religion.'

Religion in Ireland in fact always means both more and less than is evident to the outsider. It tends to determine one's education, one's social environment, one's choice of a marriage partner, even to some extent one's career in life. It is essential information between neighbours. 'Who bought the house next door ?' 'Somebody named Barber.' And an inner voice comments : 'Barber . . . that's a very Protestant name.'

On the other hand knowledge does not necessarily imply discrimination. It is no more than, so to speak, a marking-out of the white lines on the court on which the game of society will be played.

* * *

My purpose in this book is to hold up the mirror to my own

tribe, or rather that remnant of it which survives in modern Ireland. I hope to look at it with the eye of the present in the framework of the past; to examine the nature of its separate culture and to define the place which it occupies in Irish society; to ask, ultimately, whether a Protestant minority can hope to retain an identity of its own in an overwhelmingly Catholic Ireland.

In my use of the term 'Catholic' I follow the common usage: nobody outside Ulster speaks of 'Roman Catholics'. In doing so I am not, I hope, insensitive to the feelings of those purists in the Church of Ireland who reject any term which would appear to exclude them from the Catholic (i.e. the 'universal') Church. If I do not share this sensitivity, I share their objection to being defined by a negative, as 'non-Catholic'. I have used the word Anglican from time to time, for want of a better collective noun, to cover members of the Church of Ireland. It is accurate enough, but not in common usage: to those with Low Church inclinations it may still carry a whiff of incense. In a book which is concerned with people, rather than with religious institutions or religious creeds, I have had to settle for the convenient tribal terms; and I am mindful of the warning note left by Shaw:

> In Ireland all that the member of the Irish Protestant Church knows is that he is not a Roman Catholic. . . . The clause in the Apostles' Creed professing belief in a Catholic Church is a standing puzzle to Protestant children.

Roman Catholics are therefore called Catholic, except where more formal definition appears to be required. The term Protestant, again in accordance with normal usage, covers the Church of Ireland, the Presbyterians, the Methodists, and all the Nonconformist sects.

* * *

One more word of personal explanation. I was born, as I have said, a Protestant in Ireland. I am a Protestant within Shaw's definition of Protestantism—as 'a great historic movement of Reformation, Aspiration and Self-Assertion against spiritual tyrannies'. I am Irish, in a sense, by choice: both my parents happened to be English, but I have never thought of myself, from the age of fourteen, as anything but an Irishman. I offer this information in case others find it relevant, since I find it better to define the subjective eye than to pretend to objectivity.

Jack White, January 1975

I

The Five per Cent

ONE hundred years ago Protestants in Ireland numbered rather more than one to every four Catholics. Today the proportions are not very different, although a century of emigration has reduced the numbers. In fact the minority has slightly improved its position. In the census of 1861 the persons who declared a religion 'other than Roman Catholic' came to just over 22 per cent. In 1961 the proportion was over 25 per cent.*

But these are the figures for the whole island of Ireland. In 1920 the Government of Ireland Act severed from the thirty-two counties of Ireland the six which had the highest concentration of Protestants. Looking at the twenty-six counties which became the Irish Free State (and subsequently the Republic of Ireland) we see a rather different picture.

In a hundred years the population of this territory has fallen from around 4,500,000 to 2,800,000. In 1861 Protestants numbered 10·6 per cent of the total population. In 1961 they made up only 5·1 per cent. In numerical terms their strength had fallen from 466,000 to 144,868. During the first fifty years—from 1861 to 1911—there was no significant difference in the rate of decline of the two principal religious groups. The same pressures affected them both, though in different degrees: Victorian families were large and farms were small. By 1911 Protestants still numbered about 10 per cent of the reduced population. But over the next fifteen years—the years that saw the Great War, the 1916 Rising, the Anglo-Irish War and the birth of the Free State—the decline

* As this chapter was in preparation the Central Statistics Office produced the preliminary results for the census of 1971. The two tables on religion confirm the general trends of the 1961 census, revealing a further drop in the Protestant population. Pending a full analysis of the 1971 data, however, I have based this chapter on the published results of 1961. In the final paragraphs I have made some comments on the available figures for 1971.

was catastrophic. The Protestant population went down by 32·5 per cent—almost one-third—while the Catholics declined by a nominal 2·2 per cent.

* * *

It is not easy to assess the effect of the Great War in numerical terms; but if one may make an emotional judgment, it is that the war cut a wound deep into the heart of Protestant Ireland— a wound from which it never recovered. There is no parish church in the country that does not have on its wall a tablet carved with the Roll of Honour—'to the men of this parish who gave their lives in the Great War, 1914–18'. At St Paul's, in the centre of Dublin, the roll runs to forty-seven names. At Midleton—where the total Church of Ireland population, in all age-groups, was around seventy—there are eight names. In parishes where members were counted in hundreds, at best, the loss of so much young blood must have debilitated the whole community.

Not all those who were lost were casualties of the battlefield. There were many who survived the fighting, to be demobilised after the armistice, and who looked back at the Ireland of the period and decided that it was no place for a Protestant. They had always been taught to regard the whole Empire as their homeland, so it was no great hardship to seek a new future in Canada or Australia. Because there are no census figures between 1911 and 1926 it is impossible to say whether the rate of decline became sharper after independence. But it is clear enough that, over the fifteen years, the losses were great enough to alter the whole character of the Protestant community.

This change in the character of life can best be appreciated by looking at the decline in the Protestant population of individual towns and districts over the period 1911–26. In the city of Cork the drop was nearly 50 per cent. In Midleton—a marketing centre for the farmers of East Cork—it was almost 60 per cent. By 1926 the *total* number of Protestants in Midleton was 44 persons in a town of 2,700. At Fermoy, in the north of the county, the drop was no less than 93 per cent; but this was a special case. Fermoy was a garrison town, with a large military barracks, and the figures obviously reflect the withdrawal of the British Army after 1922.

In all cases we can see that the decline is much greater in the towns than in the associated rural districts. In Midleton rural district the decline was 23 per cent, in Fermoy rural district just over 50 per cent. In Bandon town the drop was 45 per cent, in the rural district 34 per cent. In fact the families associated with the land seem to have been the most tenacious. The landlords and the big farmers tended to move out; but the farmers who owned between fifty and five hundred acres seem to have hung on. This is the case even in the area of Bandon, which was the centre of some very ugly incidents during the 'Troubles'— incidents which, in the eyes of local Protestants, were part of a terror campaign aimed at driving them off the land. The bigger fall must have taken place among Protestants in business— especially, no doubt, those who depended for a large part of their trade on the landlord or the troops—as well as among government inspectors and other *fonctionnaires*.

The change in character affected Dublin, no less than the smaller towns. From 1829, says Dr R. B. McDowell, 'Dublin began to change from a predominantly Protestant to a predominantly Catholic city'.[1] In 1861 Protestants still numbered about 25 per cent. By 1911 they had fallen to 17 per cent, but they still made up a large and varied community. Dublin had nearly as great a variety of religious sects as Belfast boasts today. The census lists eight-five different sects or beliefs under the heading 'Other than Roman Catholic', and of these nearly seventy are Protestants of one kind or another.

By 1926 there was only one Protestant among every ten Dubliners. In some of the older suburbs, strongholds of a solid middle class, the tribe had held its position: 33 per cent in Rathmines and Rathgar, 24 per cent in Dun Laoghaire (which they still called Kingstown), 23 per cent in Pembroke, 22 per cent in Blackrock. Over the whole area of the city and suburbs the average worked out at just over 14 per cent. But the overriding fact was that in fifteen years there were 15 per cent more Catholics and 31 per cent fewer Protestants. The main casualty, so far as one can judge, had been the Protestant working man.

There was still one township where the minority retained a majority. In Greystones, Co. Wicklow, a seaside resort much favoured by retired colonels and their ladies, the Protestants could claim 57 per cent—915 persons—against 679 Catholics. It was a last bastion, and crumbling fast.

* * *

High emigration and a low birth rate continued the decline through the twenty years from 1926 to 1946. Throughout this period the emigration rate among Protestants was higher than among Catholics, and the large number of children included indicates the departure of whole families.

Emigration is part of a diminishing spiral: those who leave tend to be the younger and more vigorous members of the community, to whom one would look to produce the next generation. In the case of Catholics this deflationary process has been offset to some extent by the high fertility of the young women who remain. Protestants, with fewer women of child-bearing age and lower fertility, have been unable to meet the deficit caused by emigration. The overall consequence was a drop of 24 per cent in the Protestant population between 1926 and 1946.

After 1946 the country ran into the great post-war wave of emigration, which continued through the depressed years of the 1950s. Catholic emigration rose sharply, outstripping the rate for Protestants. Even so, the decline among Protestants continued to be faster. In the fifteen years from 1946 to 1961 the Catholic population declined by only 4 per cent, while the Protestants suffered a loss of 27,000 persons, or over 17 per cent. By 1961 emigration had ceased to be a major factor: evidently more young Protestants were prepared to stay and seek a living in their own country. One may put this down partly to a change in the social climate (though this has been more marked in the years since 1961), and partly to increased job-opportunities. In particular, economic development has created better opportunities for those with second-level education.

Essentially, then, the decline of the Protestants is due, quite simply, to their failure to reproduce the species. In 1960–62 the birth rate (for married women aged 15–44) was, for Catholics, 254·6 per thousand; for Protestants, 151·3 per thousand. (For both religious groups, incidentally, the birth rate was markedly *higher* in Northern Ireland, where contraceptives were legally available, than in the Republic, where they were not.) Catholic families were on average 50 per cent larger than Protestant families, and this differential was maintained right across occupational and social groups. The Protestant birth rate was, with one marginal exception, the lowest in the world.

Looking at the community as a whole, Protestants have fewer

children and more old people. Taking ten persons from each community, we can analyse them like this:

	Children	Adults	Over-65s
Catholics	× × ×	× × × × × ×	×
Protestants	× ×	× × × × × ×	× ×

A breakdown of the Protestants by age-groups is revealing:

	Under 14	15–64	Over 65
1926	47,100	136,700	24,200
1961	27,200	80,000	22,900

This is a picture of a population growing older, a population failing to produce enough new growth to replace the withered branches. The prognosis must be gloomy. In the words of Dr Brendan Walsh of the Economic and Social Research Institute: 'Any population which experiences a substantial natural *decrease* over a fifteen-year period . . . is obviously in serious danger of eventual extinction.'[2]

* * *

For the young man or woman who wants to marry within the tribe the prospects are not encouraging. Carlow is a prosperous Leinster county with something more than the national average proportion of Protestants (6·5 per cent). In 1961 there were in all almost 3,500 young people of what one may consider the prime marrying age—between 20 and 29. Of these 193 were Protestants: 94 men, 99 girls. Thirteen of the men and 42 of the women were already married. That left 81 Protestant bachelors to seek their soul-mates among 57 girls of their own religion— in a county of 33,000 people. In many parts of the south and west the marriage propects are even poorer. Co. Clare has a population of some 38,000. In the age-group 20–29 there were, in 1961, 42 Protestant men and 29 women. Ten of the men and 14 of the women were married. That left 32 Protestant bachelors chasing fifteen girls.

The first consequence is that many men go unmarried. Every country parson is familiar with the half-dozen or so middle-aged bachelors in his congregation : decent men, steady and industrious, regular churchgoers; brought up by their mothers 'not to drink, smoke, or marry a Catholic'; and therefore left unmarried, past the age of marrying, the end of their line. In the 1961 census over 60 per cent of Protestant males between the ages of 20 and 40 were shown as unmarried : approximately 10,000 out of a total of 16,000. Of 4,286 men between the ages of 20 and 24, only 269 were married. Women had better chances, or made more use of them. In the same age-group, 20 to 40, only about 40 per cent were single. But Protestant caution shows up when we divide the age-group : of the women between 20 and 30 only 43 per cent were married; of these between 30 and 40 the number married was 76 per cent. This age-pattern naturally has its effect on child-bearing.

In a young generation, which pays less attention to religious taboos, there is an increasing tendency for boys and girls to look for partners outside their own tribe. There are no official statistics of mixed marriages—that is, marriages between a Protestant partner and a Catholic partner—but Dr Brendan Walsh has estimated that in 1961 about 200 grooms and 125 brides of Protestant origins were married to Catholic partners. This would mean that almost 30 per cent of all Protestant grooms and 20 per cent of Protestant brides married Catholics.

The principle of the Roman Catholic Church (though it is subject to qualification, as we shall see later) is that the children of a mixed marriage shall be brought up as Catholics. This means in effect that when any Protestant marries a Catholic, the family is lost to the Protestant community. Of course, the rules are not always kept, and there are some cases of movement the other way; but generally social pressure (and, let it be admitted, the fact that the Protestant partner is more often indifferent) ensures that the couple abide by the rules of the church.

The mixed marriage is a constant source of worry to every parish clergyman, and to most Protestant parents. No single cause contributes so much to the continuing division in Irish life. There is every reason, however, to suppose that the sapping away of the community by this means will continue. Dr Howard Robinson, reporting on a recent survey in Co. Kerry (the diocese of Ardfert), writes:

It is of little wonder, however, that nearly one-sixth of the married men have chosen Roman Catholic wives. In the core of the diocese bordered by Tralee and Killarney and including Ballymacelligott and Kilcolman there remain just enough Church members to form a viable community where men can still have some hope of finding wives from among their fellow church people. Half of the single girls of the most eligible age group (22 to 26) are in Kilcolman. In the almost deserted parishes which form the perimeter of the diocese, Kilnaughtin, Dingle, Kenmare and Dromod, the numbers have fallen so low that Church members must perforce look outside their own numbers for spouses, and here more and more mixed marriages would seem inevitable.[3]

* * *

The outline figures for the 1971 census (given in a table at the end of this chapter) indicate a continuing drop in the Protestant population, compared with a slight rise in the number of Catholics. There is, however, one new aspect of the figures which calls for comment. It comes at the end of the tables:

	1961	1971
No religion	1,107	7,626
No information supplied	5,625	46,707

Taking the two categories together, we see that the number of people who declare no attachment to a church has risen from 6,732 in 1961 to 54,333 in 1971: to a total, in other words, more than 50 per cent of the strength of the Church of Ireland, and considerably more than three times the strength of the Presbyterians.

Without more information it is impossible to elucidate the meaning of these figures. How many people genuinely have no religious attachment? How many are simply telling the census official to mind his own business? But if even one-fifth of this group are Protestant by tribal origin, then a good many of one's assumptions about the decline of the tribe come into question. If, for instance, non-Protestants insist on sending their children to Protestant schools, they will have a perceptible effect on the denominational schooling system. There is at least the intimation of a trend here that may have a significance beyond statistics.

Distribution of Religious Groups		
	1961	1971
Catholics	2,673,473	2,795,596
	95·05%	95·36%
All Protestants	134,881	125,674
	4·80%	4·28%
Church of Ireland	104,016	97,741
	3·70%	3·33%
Presbyterians	18,953	16,054
	0·67%	0·55%
Methodists	6,676	5,646
	0·24%	0·19%
Society of Friends	727	647
	0·03%	0·02%
Baptists	481	591
	0·02%	0·02%
Lutherans	401	755
	0·01%	0·03%
Other religious denominations	3,627	4,250
	0·13%	0·14%

Note Small increases in the number of Lutherans and Baptists are probably explained by immigration. The 'Other religious denominations' have all been included in the total for 'All Protestants'.

2

Colonies

West Cork: Hibernian Anglicans

The classic picture of Irish rural life about the turn of the
century has been given by Somerville and Ross. Edith Somerville
and her cousin were manifestly of the Ascendancy. The Somerville village of Castletownshend, in West Cork, was an Anglo-
Irish enclave. Even today it retains, like a perfect antique, some
of that character. The tablets on the wall of the parish church
commemorate the interlocked dynasties of Somerville, Coghill
and Townshend. They lived a double life—landed gentry at
home, captains and colonels and admirals abroad. Ireland was
their home, but they went to school in England and they gave
the prime of their lives to the fleets and armies of the Empire.
They returned, if they survived the wars, to die in Cork.

All about them there lived a class of people who went to the
same church and shared the same loyalties, but never belonged
to the Ascendancy and never aspired to belong to it. They have
somehow found no record in a literary world peopled by
Protestant gentlemen and Catholic peasants. At home they were
small farmers; abroad, they were private soldiers in the Coghill
regiments, able seamen in the Somerville ships. They may be
of English origin, but they are not Anglo-Irish: unless four
centuries should be too short a time for naturalisation.

* * *

The church at The Altar, near Goleen, stands on the edge of
the sea, about twenty miles short of the Mizen Head. It is a
plain little building, designed by the local rector and built by
direct labour as famine relief. It was locally known as Teampall
na mBocht—the Church of the Poor.

On a fine Sunday morning in February the wind is ripping
in over the bay, carrying a strong smell of seaweed from the

rocks near low-water mark. From the church gate, if you look
into the wind, you have a view across a jagged inlet broken by
rocks to the mountains near the Mizen. There is scarcely a
house in sight. Outside in the road there are nineteen cars and a
couple of motor cycles. Inside, the congregation numbers about
sixty. In summer there might be tourists among them, but at this
time of year they are all residents. They are carefully dressed,
in sober Sunday clothes, but the men have that deeply weather-
beaten look that marks out the farmer or the fisherman.

The church interior is as austere as a Baptist chapel, but for
a single stained-glass window at the east end. The rector
preaches to the text 'The Lord hath made all things new', and
talks about the coming of spring. The small choir leads the
singing of 'All Things Bright and Beautiful'.

In the graveyard there are clusters of artificial flowers under
glass domes on the newer graves. The headstones give a roll-
call of local names: Levis, Swanton, Roycroft, Jermyn, Hunt,
Pyburn, Attridge, Allen, Connell, Hegarty. But no eye could
be sharp enough to distinguish the Allens and Roycrofts who
file out after service, into the clean cold air, from the McCarthys
and O'Sullivans who are standing around and chatting after
mass outside the Catholic church at Goleen, a couple of miles
away.

* * *

'This', wrote a clerical gentleman, 'is a typical Irish parish,
the softening and elevating influence of a resident gentry being
wholly wanting.'[1] The root-stock must be the settlers who were
brought in by the Earls of Bandon when they succeeded (by
confiscation, the usual title) to the vast O'Mahony estates after
the Desmond Rebellion at the end of the sixteenth century.
Probably the strain has been mixed with a good deal of Irish
blood, but not many distinctively Irish names appear on the
parish rolls: of 64 families, sharing 35 names, only seven names
have strong Irish associations. It would be too simple, of course,
to date all others back to the planters. Crookhaven, a few miles
west along the coast, was an important port in the days of sail—
the first landfall for windjammers as they sailed in from the
Atlantic. It must have been a kind of inlet through which other
people came to settle. One can imagine sailors leaving their
ships and marrying Irish wives. Roycrofts rowed their own boat

ashore—the story goes—from a Spanish ship: dark hair and dark eyes persist in the family to this day, Pyburns came as boat builders from Wales. Dukelow (Du Clos?) and Camier must be Huguenots, possibly refugees who came by way of the direct ships from the continent. Of the young men, many returned to sea, with the British Navy. We may form a picture of a colony without an aristocracy, a colony which looked for its associations with the world to the sea rather than the land.

In 1911 the parishes of Goleen and The Altar together numbered about a thousand people. Today the total for the combined parish (Kilmoe Union) is about two hundred. By the standards of Irish Protestants they are not a very small minority. The proportion of 'non-Catholics' in this rural district runs to 15 or 16 per cent. And in spite of their small numbers, there seem to be enough of them to create a sense of community. Sunday morning service at The Altar has a pleasing sense of a family occasion. Their sense of community must owe something to the fact that they are almost all small farmers. Their average holding is probably 'the grass of ten cows', which would mean, in cash terms, an income of £1,000–£1,500 a year.

In absolute terms the community has not been declining over, say, the last ten years, but the figures are misleading. The decline of the native-born has been counterbalanced by the arrival of immigrants, mostly English and German. About forty houses have been taken over and kept alive by such new arrivals. But in the main they are only summer residents, and they do not help the demographic structure of the native Protestant population.

The national pattern is shown here on a local scale. Of 200 parishioners, over 60 are more than 60 years of age (30 per cent). Of the over-35s, 65 are unmarried (32½ per cent). There seems to be a pattern of older men marrying younger women—in some cases the gap is as much as twenty years. In this the Protestants are probably not much different from their Catholic neighbours: it is customary enough for a man to wait until his parents are dead before he thinks of marriage, and then his eye is likely to be taken by a younger woman. There are some signs that this marriage pattern is changing, and parents, with an eye to the future, are beginning to look more benevolently on early marriages.

Marriage customs have been very much bound up, in the past anyway, with a tribal sense of land-ownership. Mixed marriages have been frowned on partly because they tended to let land and property slip into the hands of the Other Side. Within the community, therefore, intermarriage has been very important: the complexity of cousinships is astonishing. One farmer—an only son of an only son—maintains that these customs have led to bad breeding, in the genetic sense:

A Protestant farmer always likes his son to marry an heiress —a girl who will be coming into a farm or a fortune in her own right. But if a girl is sole heir, it often means that the breed is one that doesn't reproduce well in the male line. . . .

Seventy years ago Kilmoe had five large Protestant primary schools. Only one now survives, and the future of this is bound to be in question. On the roll, at the time of writing, there are eighteen pupils, aged from five to thirteen, under one teacher. Since the coming of free education at least 60 per cent of these will want to go on to second-level education. They must, however, face a problem: there is no Protestant secondary school nearer than Bandon, sixty miles away. If they wish to remain within the Protestant fold, therefore, they must go away as boarders, paying fees that are now more than £300 a year.

The alternative is to go daily to Skibbereen, to the convent or the vocational school. At the convent they are exempted as a matter of course from all Catholic observance, and a local clergyman comes in to give them religious instruction. The vocational school is non-denominational, but it too has, of course, a vast majority of Catholic pupils. With boarding school fees rising fast, and religious distinction appearing less vital, parents may be increasingly inclined to accept the risks—whatever they are— of desegregation.

* * *

For the outsider it is difficult to disentangle the complex threads of social relationships. The traditional neighbourliness of the countryside overrides religious distinctions. Farmers have always got together to help one another at threshing time; Catholic and Protestants have always attended one another's wakes. The Protestant community lived through a period of tension during the Troubles, when the whole of West Cork was a

theatre of action, because their sympathies were well known:
'We were very British at that time, most of the Protestant people
were very British.' One can hear an echo of old fears when a
schoolboy says: 'You'd mind what you're saying. . . . You never
push your luck. . . .' In general, however, Protestants have been
joining increasingly with their neighbours in the activities of the
area. Farm-based associations have been particularly fruitful in
developing a spirit of neighbourly co-operation. Protestants are
active in Macra na Feirme (the young farmers' society), in the
Irish Farmers' Association and in the Irish Countrywomen's
Association, and their activities in such groups tend towards a
wider desegregation of social life.

The future of the parish is of course uncertain. There is no
cheer in the figures for baptisms, marriages and burials, ex-
tracted from the parish register for each decade since 1901.

	Baptisms	Marriages	Burials
1901–10	133	19	63
1910–20	86	28	74
1921–30	54	28	52
1931–40* 1941–50* 1951–60*	36	7	60
1961–70	18	6	40

* Figures given to me as a total for the thirty years. I have divided by
three to give the ten-year average.

In brief: in the decade 1901–10 baptisms outnumbered
burials by more than two to one. Now burials outnumber
baptisms by something like the same proportion.

Monaghan: The Ulster Scots

The town of Clones lies right on the border, a small commercial centre—2,000 people or so—set among the hilly farms
of north-west Monaghan. Before partition its hinterland lay
largely in the neighbouring county of Fermanagh, and its trade-

routes led towards Belfast. Every morning, even now, the news-agent gets a bundle of the *Belfast Newsletter*.

Older Protestants here have felt for fifty years 'like Northerners in exile'. In speech, in character, in style of life they are recognisably Ulster Scots, from the stock of the plantations. Many have family links with the North, and they have constant contact still in church affairs: the Presbyterian minister serves congregations in Fermanagh as well as Monaghan, and the Church of Ireland diocese of Clogher straddles the border.

When the partition settlement was made three Ulster counties —Monaghan, Cavan and Donegal—fell to the Free State. The other six became the statelet of Northern Ireland. It was a settlement that filled the loyalists of Monaghan with indignation. 'We felt', one of them told me, 'that we had been thrown to the wolves.' They formed the Protestant Association 'to protect our interests, to see we got fair play'. Nobody is quite sure, by now, exactly what specifically Protestant interests the Association is designed to protect; but it still nominates candidates for the local elections, and in 1974 had enough voting-power to get two of its candidates elected.

This stern and stony county has had a high rate of emigration for a century. It had a population of over 100,000 in 1881 and has under 50,000 today. Farms have never been rich, and in the last fifty years commercial life has been smothered by the border. Even so, Protestants have lost more heavily than Catholics. In 1911 they made up 25 per cent of the population; today the proportion has fallen to 14 per cent. The Church of Ireland rector of Clones ministers to about 130. The Presbyterian minister has about 100, but they are in three congregations, one of which lies across the border. In the town of Clones Protestants make up only 10 per cent, and a local man said that he could recall most of the principal businesses changing from Protestant to Catholic hands within his memory. In the surrounding countryside, however, the Protestant population is up to 30 per cent. Here the Presbyterians have an edge over the Church of Ireland, in terms of numbers, and it is the Presbyterian ethos—the ethos of the Ulster Scot—that dominates the community. Sunday is a day for church and for visiting relatives, but not for sport or entertainment; nor, of course, for any work that is not absolutely necessary. A good Protestant farmer will milk his cows on Sunday, because that must be done, but he will not make hay on a Sunday—even if Sunday happens to be the only dry day in a wet season. There is a deep-rooted belief in the puritan virtues of industry and thrift; and with it goes a sense that such virtues are peculiar to Protestants. A housewife is expected to be a 'good manager', which means that she will have a spotless house and handle money thriftily, but will always have a cake and fresh scones to put on the table for a visitor.

* * *

In an area like this, right on the border, one can expect the troubles in the North to be reflected in tensions in the community. Among the Protestants the older people, at least, share in the Ulster loyalist's intense devotion to the Crown. 'A lot of them', a younger man said wryly, 'seem to think that the Queen is part of the Protestant religion.' The bonds are strengthened by family links across the border. And proximity becomes real when a bomb goes up in Fivemiletown and the windows rattle in Clones.

Catholics too have sympathies with the people across the border, but to them the phrase 'our people in the North' tends to mean the minority, Catholic in religion and nationalist in sentiment. Such a disparity of allegiance must lead to some constraints—if only a habit of not talking until you know who you are talking to. Nevertheless, neighbourly relations seem to follow the traditional rural patterns. A Presbyterian farmer with a biggish farm only a couple of miles from the border says he is on excellent terms with his neighbours, even though 'they all know where I stand'.

A few years ago I had a very bad accident and I had to be rushed up to Dublin to hospital. . . . While I was away, thirteen of my neighbours came in, quite spontaneously, to do the work. They harvested my corn for me and did all the work of the farm, even though my wife was in Dublin and there was nobody in the house at the time. Nearly all of those were Catholics, and one of them is the biggest IRA man in the district.

A Catholic, not far away, says that relations are amicable enough, but superficial. He knows the men of the other tribe because they go to the cattle mart and to meetings of the farmers' association, but his wife knows hardly any of their wives. He puts this down less to sectarianism than to a difference in social habits.

> If I go to call on Mrs —— [a Catholic], I know that she'll ask me into the kitchen right away. . . . If I call at a Protestant house, they'll be quite friendly, but we'll probably talk on the doorstep.

Catholics see Protestants as formal and a little chilly. Protestants see Catholics as basically unreliable : not just politically but in their essential character.

* * *

Probably the older people will never quite lose the feeling that in 1922 the doors of the ark closed and they were left outside :

> The fellow down here has much the same outlook as the fellow in the North. . . . We are suspicious of the Roman Catholic Church; we think it has too much influence in this country.

The younger people are beginning to think of themselves as citizens of an Irish Republic. With a general increase in prosperity, they are losing the old hopeless feeling that the only future lies in emigration, and to stay at home is failure. There are about sixty-five children in the Protestant national school. For secondary education they can go to the Collegiate School in Monaghan, with the aid of a bus service provided by the state. But some families send their children across the border to Newtownbutler. The reason they give, generally, is that 'there's no use in them learning Irish, they'll never get anything here anyway'. But underlying this may be the ingrained belief that everything in the North is better. One outspoken Protestant thinks they should stay :

> What's to stop them learning Irish; it's no different from any other subject, French or anything else. They should stand their ground and learn the Irish and put in for the jobs; and then if they don't get them we'll know the reason.

'Stand their ground' : it is a very characteristic phrase, suggestive of a people who value stubborn tenacity above flexibility or originality.

Tipperary: The Enthusiasts

The village of Cloughjordan lies among the rich farmland of north Tipperary, not far from the town of Nenagh. It is a quiet, straggling little place, on the main road to nowhere. During the railway age it had a minor commercial importance as a centre of distribution, but the railway has declined and there has been no industrial development to replace it as a source of employment. The shops in the main street still wear an authentic rural air : they have not yet put on the uniform of the supermarket chains. But there are three substantial churches —Catholic, Church of Ireland and Methodist. For this corner of Tipperary has been for two hundred years the centre of a little colony of Methodists.

The Cloughjordan district was settled after the Cromwellian wars with disbanded soldiers. Like many settlers of puritan stock, they probably looked with disfavour on the laxity of the Established Church, and welcomed the Wesleyan 'enthusiasm' as a revival of the true faith. Wesley himself did not preach in the village, but it was visited as early as 1755 by one of his famous itinerant preachers, Thomas Walsh. Walsh was a native Irish speaker, so he was able to preach to the country people in their own tongue. On his first visit to Cloughjordan he was showered with stones and mud; but he must have sown a seed, for Methodist services were being held regularly in the village by 1793.

The history of Methodism in the district is particularly bound up with the Armitage family. Of the forty families in the congregation perhaps fifteen bear the name of Armitage, and as many are connected with it by marriage. Its dynasties are so complicated that members must be identified by the names of their properties—'Jim of Lissadonagh'. The first Armitages came from Yorkshire, and seem to have arrived in Tipperary during the seventeenth century. They made their lives very much within their own colony : generally they married Methodists, and by careful match-making they kept their farms and fortunes within the family circle. Until quite recently they were strictly loyal to their puritan tradition : Sunday meant church and a good dinner, but menial jobs like shining shoes and drawing water were completed on Saturday, and farm work was out of the question.

Down to the present generation the Cloughjordan Methodists have remained farmers. They are industrious and self-reliant, and have built up and consolidated their farms. In general their holdings lie in the comfortable but not affluent bracket. Their income is invested very heavily in the education of their children. There is a local primary school, but for secondary education the choice lies between Limerick and Dublin. Those who can afford the fees send their sons and daughters to Wesley College in Dublin—the largest privately managed Protestant secondary school in the Republic, and co-educational since 1912. But fees for boarders run (in 1975) around £600 a year—plus fares, of course, and all other extras; so for a middling farmer with three or four children, even given the help of state grants, the burden can be heavy.

A few nowadays go to the Catholic schools in Nenagh. Others go to Gorteen Agricultural College, not far away, which is a Methodist foundation. Most of these will return to farming, with the advantage of a training in the science and skills of agriculture. But of the boys and girls who go to Dublin, a fair proportion will move into business or the professions—the careers of urban society—and will be lost to the community for ever.

As a whole this little community seems to have moved into the era of national independence without any great sense of shock or insecurity. Interdenominational relationships are good, and Methodist farmers and their wives are active in the rural organisations. At the same time, the social pattern is a pattern of distinct communities. Even the Methodists and the Church of Ireland parishioners lead somewhat separate lives. Their young get together for table tennis, badminton and dancing, but all these activities are for Protestants only; and parents say they will maintain segregation until the Catholic Church modifies its stand on mixed marriages.

> As it stands, if one of our boys or girls makes a mixed marriage, that's a whole family lost to the church. Naturally we'll try to prevent that if we can.

A colony of forty families cannot afford many losses.

Dublin: Protestant Pluralism

In the year 1213 the Archbishop Henry de Londres advanced the Collegiate Church of St Patrick, just outside Dublin, to the status of a cathedral. He did so principally, it seems, to spite the clergy of Christ Church, which occupied a small mound within the city walls, just 450 paces away. With the Reformation both buildings passed over to the new order, and both remain as cathedrals of the Church of Ireland to the present day.

Even in 1213 the citizen of Dublin may well have wondered if the city needed two cathedrals. In 1975 the tower of Christ Church and the steeple of St Patrick's stand—only a decent golf-drive apart—like two ancient fortresses guarding an abandoned frontier. Inside the bugle sounds, the colours fly, the garrison forms fours. But the war, if there is a war, is going on somewhere else.

* * *

Dublin is still the city that the Ascendancy made. The finest of its buildings date back to an era of despotic government by Protestant grandees. Their names survive—where those of patriots have not supplanted them—on streets and squares. They left the city with the strong skeleton of dignified thorough-fares which still supports, somehow or other, the adipose tissue of the mid-twentieth century.

This was the capital of a colonial society; these were its rulers. They were marked off from the people they ruled by their religion, as surely as the savage was marked off by the colour of his skin. But their own tribe was divided within itself even then, and is much more divided today, and each sub-tribe has its own identity, its own institutions, its own monuments.

Dissent is not much less ancient in the city than the Reformation itself. There was a Presbyterian congregation in the 1640s. Quaker meetings were held from about 1654. Methodist preachers gathered their first meetings a couple of years before John Wesley made his first visit in 1747. They were responsible, in a way, for a nickname that has been handed down through generations of Dublin schoolboys, as a slightly derogatory name for Protestants: an ignorant priest, hearing a preacher speak of 'the babe in swaddling clothes', dubbed the new sect 'Swaddlers'. The evangelical revival of the nineteenth century brought new sub-divisions. The Plymouth Brethren, so-called, had their origin in Wicklow, and held their first meetings in Dublin before 1830. The Salvation Army came in 1880, with its brass bands and its uniforms; the fifty or sixty members still follow the tradition of Major Barbara, beating out hymns at street-corners and giving food and shelter to the needy at their hostel.

More than one-third of all the Protestants in the Republic live in the area of Dublin city and county. The census counts some 38,000 members of the Church of Ireland, and about 7,500 Presbyterians and Methodists. Other denominations make up perhaps a couple of thousand.* The Saturday *Irish Times* lists two cathedrals and about forty parish churches, nine or ten Presbyterian churches and about the same for Methodists; as well as one Moravian, two Baptist, one Congregational, six or seven gospel halls, and various meetings of the Society of Friends.

All these varieties of Protestant are, in a sense, the sub-tribes of a single tribe. They attend (or at least enrol themselves under) different churches, but they go to the same schools, they use the same institutions, they intermarry : they filter, generation by generation, into one another. Still, all told, they number not much more than one in twenty of the population in the exended city.

* * *

With the growth of the city the Protestant population moves outwards in ever-extending rings; churches and schools are full in the outer suburbs, while the centre is gradually being abandoned. At North Strand parish, in the grey streets behind the docks and the railway, the members used to number upwards of 4,000. Now they are down to 1,500. Their character is changing too. Once the majority of the households depended on the ships, the trains and the warehouses; it was the world of the 'poor Protestants', the men like Seán O'Casey. Nowadays there are fewer overalls and more white collars, but it is still far from the world of the affluent Protestant : fewer than half the families, for instance, run a motor-car.

A good many of the parishioners were born and raised in the area, went to the church school, found their entertainment and did their courting at the church hall. But the boys and girls

---

* These figures are estimates based on guesswork : the census categorises nearly 10,000 as 'Others, including no statement'.

who are growing up now do not limit their social lives as their parents did. They mix with Catholics at work; they go out with Catholics; often they marry Catholics. Every second engagement, I am informed, is to a Catholic.

Mixed or not, marriage is likely to take the young people out of the parish. Instead of settling into the red-brick terraces where they grew up, they take off to the new estates in the suburbs. To Dundrum, perhaps, where the parish school has four hundred pupils, and Wesley College is just up the hill. Or to Kill o' the Grange, where a resident one Sunday morning looked into a church that was packed from wall to wall, and complained : 'You might as well be going to mass !'

* * *

Thirty years ago Lucan was a village to the west of Dublin. Now, if you stand on the hill, you see the church tower across a valley filled with the roofs of new houses. Parks, Groves, Lawns and Avenues of bright semi-detached villas clamber all over the hillsides.

In a parish like this you can feel, the rector says, that 'the tide is coming in'. There are about 150 families, totalling some 400 men, women and children. The number has doubled in the past seven years. Most are married couples under forty with young families. They work in banks or in business, and earn good middle-bracket incomes; but when they have coped with the mortgage on the house and the payments on the car, they have no great surplus of spending-money. Most of them send their children to the national school managed by the rector. For secondary schooling the majority, both boys and girls, will go down the road to the King's Hospital : that will mean school fees (£150 a year for day pupils) on top of the hire-purchase and the mortgage. There is no evidence of enthusiasm for desegregation : 'There was talk of a community school here but the idea was dropped—nobody wanted it.'

The social pattern here is the pattern of the commuter belt. Most parishioners work in Dublin, alongside Catholic colleagues, and they feel no particular interest in social activities for Protestants alone. A young vestryman thought that desegregated schooling was unthinkable as long as the Catholic Church maintained its rules on mixed marriages, but he had no sense of discrimination.

We've had fair play, certainly, but why not? By and large
the Protestants are an industrious group. . . . We have a tradition of integrity and honour, and that's still relevant. We play
our part in this country. I don't think we would ever feel
anything but Irish.

3
'Cromwell's Greedy Gang'

IN Northern Ireland Protestant and Catholic have resolved
their origins into the common myth of the Planter and the Gael.
It is a myth in the sense that it is a communal belief : a truth
with accretions. History is never quite so tidy. Not all Catholics
are of pure Gaelic stock, nor are all Protestants the pure
descendants of Scots and English settlers. For general purposes,
all the same, the distinction is good enough. No doubt there are
thousands of Ulster Protestants who are sprung from land
stewards, railway engineers, government officials; but they have
been absorbed into the myth of the Planter. They are the boys
who kicked the Pope right over Dolly's Brae.

The origins of the Southern Protestant appear to be much
more diverse. They are not all descendants of alien land-
grabbers; they are not all, by any reasonable definition of the
term, Anglo-Irish. Shaw, who was one of them, summed up his
own origins :

> When I say that I am an Irishman I mean that I was born
> in Ireland and that my native language is English, not the
> unspeakable jargon of the mid-nineteenth-century London
> newspapers. My extraction is the extraction of most English-
> men; that is, I have no trace in me of the commercially im-
> ported North Spanish strain which passes for aboriginal Irish.
> I am a genuine typical Irishman of the Danish, Norman,
> Cromwellian and (of course) Scotch invasions.[1]

Some of the best known Protestant families can trace their
descent from the clans of pre-Norman Ireland. The O'Briens
of Clare, for instance, turned to the Established Church as early
as the reign of Henry VIII. Some—Butler, Fitzgerald, Fitz-
simons—had their origin in the Norman invaders. Many are the

relics of plantations—not only in Ulster but in Munster and the midlands. Some originated with disbanded soldiers of the Williamite wars; some with farmers, gardeners or land stewards brought in by improving landlords. On top of all this one must not overlook the close commerce between the two islands over the last 150 years : the soldiers in garrison, the district inspectors of constabulary, the Resident Magistrates, the railway officials—all that vast class of transients who came to Ireland, as they went to India, to make a career; nor the clergy themselves, who often came from England, but naturalised, so to speak, and left their offspring in Ireland.

All one can really say, as a common denominator, is that the immigrant strain is more marked among Protestants than among Catholics; and this factor underlies the dual loyalty which has constantly confused their political thinking.

* * *

There is no ambiguity about the origin of English Protestants. They are simply Englishmen who accepted the Reformation. And for the English the Reformation (in its early stages at any rate) was a national rather than a religious experience. In Ireland it bore quite a different aspect. It came as an element in a struggle with a foreign culture, its advance signalled everywhere by the advance of a foreign language. Spenser, writing from his experience as a settler in Co. Cork, found the Irish quite ignorant of the nature of Protestantism : 'And yet they do hate it, though unknown, even for the very hatred which they have for the English and their government.'[2]

But the men who governed Ireland for Elizabeth were not sent to make Ireland Protestant : they were sent to make Ireland safe. A wild, ungovernable island only fifty miles from England's coast—an island which professed fealty to the Pope rather than the Crown—was a standing invitation to Her Majesty's enemies. And, just as the Irish identified the English religion with the English government, so the English officials saw the Irish religion as one element in a total pattern of society which was incompatible with peace and security. Coming from a way of life based on a rural corn-growing economy, they saw the habits of a pastoral cattle-raising people as a prescription for anarchy. Fynes Moryson thought that society should be stabilised by more tillage and less grazing, a formula which called for tenancies on the English system. From this point it was not very difficult to argue that security for the future lay in colonisation.

The government of Mary had already created two areas of settlement (roughly Leix and Offaly) on the fringe of Leinster. Here Irish and English were to be settled side by side under English law. 'Browne and Shute and Girton, and Masterson and Jones . . . were to be settled on lands from which Irishmen were driven, and were to live in peace, side by side, with MacShane and O'Dowlyn and O'Fahy and McNeill Boy and the O'Mores.'[8] The tensions implicit in such an arrangement were soon felt, and when Elizabeth's governors determined on the plantation of Munster they used a different model. The province had been laid waste and vast numbers of its people slaughtered as part of the process of pacification by Elizabeth's generals. It was now decided to replace the Irish chiefs by a resident English gentry, settled upon land confiscated from the Munster rebels.

The plantation was not a great success. Not enough English gentlemen wanted to hazard their fortunes in the wilds of Munster; and those who received grants often found it simpler to let the land to Irish tenants than to fulfil the terms of their settlements by bringing in Englishmen. When Hugh O'Neill's forces advanced to the south towards the end of the century most of the settlers, big and small alike, were driven from their lands again. Not for the first or the last time in Irish history, the intentions of a forceful central government at Westminster were frustrated by the defective apparatus of local administration. All the same, the very difficulty of government at long range commended colonisation as a means of stabilising conquest. The formula was used again in Ulster under James I, and this time the job was done more competently. The Scots and English settlers of the period are the root-stock of Protestant Ulster.

* * *

English was the language of conquest; it could not be the language of conversion. No very zealous effort was made during Elizabeth's reign to bring the new faith to the Irish people. Spenser contrasts the idleness of the established clergy with the zeal of the popish priests: 'For they spare not to come out of Spain, from Rome, from Rheims, by long toil and dangerous travel hither, where they know peril of death awaiteth them and no reward or riches is to be found, only to draw the people to the Church of Rome.' Bishops, usually political appointments, were concerned mainly to enrich themselves, while the parish clergy lived like laymen and neglected all ministration of the gospel. By the beginning of James's reign, says Professor J. C. Beckett, the thrust of the Reformation in Ireland had already failed. The vast bulk of the people, Irish natives and Old English settlers alike, clung to the old doctrines. 'The Protestant population, though growing slowly, consisted of little more than a handful of officials and a few recent settlers.'⁴

* * *

From the death of Elizabeth to the Battle of the Boyne is a matter of less than ninety years—an old man's lifetime. Yet in that period Irish society was altered firmly and finally. The last of the chiefs who might have led a native and Catholic counter-conquest had been dispossessed, the power of the Catholic aristocracy had been broken, and the land settlements had planted in Ulster, the most turbulent of the provinces, a stubborn garrison of English and Scots Protestants. Throughout the rest of the country the native ruling class had been replaced, though the common people remained Irish and Catholic.

The settlers had been made acutely aware of their exposed position by the war of 1641. Under the leadership of their gentry, the Catholics rose in concerted rebellion and drove the new owners off the land. Protestants took refuge in castles and walled towns, and streams of destitute refugees poured into Dublin, bringing with them hair-raising stories of a popish reign of terror. Puritan pamphleteers spread the word throughout England and created in English Protestants a righteous zeal for vengeance. A century later the atrocity stories still made John Wesley's flesh creep:

> I procured a genuine account of the great Irish massacre of 1641. Surely never was there such a transaction before, from the beginning of the world! More than two hundred thousand men, women and children, butchered within a few months, in cool blood, and with such circumstances of cruelty as make one's blood run cold! It is well if God has not a controversy with the nation, on this account, to this day.⁵

Wesley's figures were, by any estimate, a wild exaggeration. A recent estimate puts the *total* Protestant population of Ulster in the mid-1620s at around 25,000; it can hardly have been more than 35,000 twenty years later. As for the casualties, the most credible figure that emerged from the controversy of the early eighteenth century was around four or five thousand. The slaughter of one in seven was, of course, a terrifying experience for the settlers; and some shadow of the terror—quite dissociated from the facts—still haunts the folk-memory of the Ulster Protestant. What Catholic Ireland remembers is different. It remembers that Cromwell stepped in on God's behalf, within a few years, to settle the account. By wholesale confiscation of land and by the introduction of a new wave of settlers—many of them disbanded soldiers of the parliamentary army—Cromwell proposed to rule out any prospect of Catholic insurrection for the future.

The Catholics had a brief revival of hope at the Restoration, but William III's victory over James II finally wrecked their chances of a successful combination against the might of the Crown. By the early part of the eighteenth century only one-seventh of the land of Ireland remained in the hands of Catholic proprietors; and that proportion was to be further reduced under the penal laws of the century that followed.

* * *

During the eighteenth century the colony was reinforced by the arrival of many place-hunters, lay and ecclesiastical. Almost all the bishops were English, and many were absentees. Revenues from some of the sees were enormous: Derry was worth £7,000 a year, Dublin and Cashel £4,000, according to Arthur Young, while 'the lands of the Primacy would, if let as a private estate, be worth near one hundred thousand pounds a year'.[6] Under such worldly prelates the Established Church displayed little missionary zeal. John Wesley, who made the first of his many visits to Ireland in 1747, found it no wonder 'that most who are born Papists generally live and die as such, when the Protestants can find no better ways to convert them than penal laws and Acts of Parliament'.[7] Indeed, it has been argued that the Protestants did not even want to convert the Catholics, because by doing so they would enlarge the circle of privilege.

The penal laws debarred Catholics from parliament and from any government office, from commissions in the army and navy, and from the legal profession, while their rights to hold land were severely limited. The effect of these provisions was that lawyers and large landowners conformed to the Established Church in considerable numbers. Overall, however, the record of conversions is unimpressive. The Convert Rolls for Co. Clare for the period 1702 to 1789 list 231 persons—an average of rather less than three a year. Most seem to have been small landowners, though there are a few merchants and tradesmen, such as 'Bolton, Peter, periwig-maker, of Ennis'.[8]

On the other hand, the Catholic Church, with all its disabilities, made headway among the Protestant settlers. Under the penal laws Catholic worship continued, but often under conditions of danger or hardship which could only arouse admiration for the devotion of the priests. The people, Arthur Young wrote, 'who had been stripped of their all, were more enraged than converted; they adhered to the persuasion of their forefathers with the steadiest and most determined zeal; while the priests . . . made proselytes among the common Protestants, in defiance of every danger'.[9] Intermarriage no doubt played its part in the process of conversion. The disbanded soldiers, in particular, had quickly shown themselves susceptible to the charms of the papist women, whom an earlier English commentator had pronounced 'well favoured, clean-coloured, fair-handed, big and large'.

* * *

The Protestant stock had been reinforced by small but significant infusions from the continent. French Huguenots, refugees from persecution in France, began to arrive in Dublin as early as 1660, and a chapel in St Patrick's Cathedral was set aside for services in the French language. They brought with them industrial and commercial talents which were of great importance in the development of their new country. As weavers they laid the foundation of poplin manufacture; as silversmiths they played a great part in the flowering of Irish silverwork during the eighteenth century; while the banking family of La Touche may claim to be the founders of the Bank of Ireland. Others, many of them disbanded soldiers coming from the wars in the Netherlands, formed colonies elsewhere under the terms of an act of parliament which provided for 'the encouragement of Protestant strangers to settle in this Kingdom of Ireland'. The colonists gradually became assimilated, but names like La Touche, Vignoles, Fleury, de Foubert still bear witness to their origins. After 1700 groups of Palatine Germans were brought in and settled by landlords who thought that their agricultural skill would improve the land and raise the standard of farming. They were settled principally in Limerick and north Kerry, where names like Shier and Bovenizer are still to be found. Young found them 'very industrious, and in consequence much happier and better fed, clothed and lodged, than the Irish peasants'; he also pointed out that 'their being independent of farmers, and having leases, are circumstances that will create industry'.

Young was an admirer of the economic virtues, and he did not stint his praise for those landlords who devoted industry and capital to the improvement of their estates. For the landlord class in general, and in particular 'the little country gentlemen, the vermin of the kingdom', he expresses nothing but scorn:

> The landlord of an Irish estate, inhabited by Roman Catholics, is a sort of despot who yields obedience, in whatever concerns the poor, to no law but that of his own will.[10]

The cure for insurrection did not lie in oppressive laws:

> Treat them like men who ought to be as free as yourselves; put an end to that system of religious persecution which for seventy years has divided the kingdom against itself: in these two circumstances lie the cure for insurrection.[11]

* * *

There were some Protestants who were prepared to listen to such counsel. After almost a century of peace and supremacy they were beginning to feel impatient of England's apron-strings. They saw that the interests of England would always be paramount at Westminster; that when Irish manufactures threatened to compete with English products, Irish industry was suppressed. They came to see that laws made in London were often quite unsuitable for application in Mayo or Tipperary. The period of Grattan's Parliament and the Irish Volunteers—less than twenty years in all—appears in retrospect as an era of unrivalled promise. The colonists had begun to discover a nationality. To be sure, the nation they conceived was a Protestant nation: it still did not embrace and it did not represent the great mass of

Irish Catholics. The nationality was not quite Irish but it was
not quite English either : for the first time, perhaps, the term
Anglo-Irish appears to have a meaning. Somehow there had
developed a sense of a distinct identity, and the beginnings of a
different culture. Almost all the fine buildings in Dublin, and
indeed throughout the country, can be traced to their time or
their inspiration. They were the patrons of the Irish crafts—
glassware, silver, plasterwork. Arland Ussher, who came of that
stock, wrote of them :

> The Georgians, at least in the finer second half of the century,
> were more than mere roisterers; they were—many of them—
> builders, landscape gardeners, fine speakers in public and
> writers in private. The evidence is there in their mansions
> —often built without the employment of a professional archi-
> tect; in the layout of their estates, in the diaries of such men
> as Barrington. They may have been British colonists—though
> they would have resented the term—but they were not provin-
> cials. They were something more than the 'Garrison' type
> from which they originated, and to which, unfortunately, they
> reverted.[12]

Revert they did. The 1798 rebellion frightened the life out
of them : all the old fears of Catholic vengeance were revived
by the peasant brutality of the Wexford rebels, and Cruik-
shank's bloodthirsty engravings carried on the tremor through
later generations. In the North, where Wolfe Tone had declared
the Presbyterians to be 'sincere and enlightened republicans', the
revolutionary spirit was extinguished, as fear of the papists
welled up again. The Union was pushed through the Irish
parliament, against determined opposition from all the best elements in that assembly, by means of votes bought with titles,
places and bribes. But within a generation Protestants great and
small were ardent loyalists. O'Connell, wielding the rude weapon
of the Catholic democracy, showed them what would happen to
their hegemony when the majority began to make its power
felt. They began to feel, as they had never felt in the eighteenth
century, a sense of minority; and from then on they looked to
England for protection.

* * *

In Mary Tudor's time there was no doubt that a Masterson

and a Jones were Protestant, an O'More and an O'Farrell were Catholic. The very names of the new settlers were the symbol of change, and were jeered at by the Gaelic poets :

Upton, Evans, Bevins, Basset is [and] Blair,
Burton, Beecher, Wheeler, Farren is Fair,
Turner, Fielding, Reeves is Wallis is Dean,
Cromwell 's a bhuidhean sain scaoileach scaipeadh ar a dtréid.
[Cromwell and his greedy gang, may his tribe be scattered][13]

Four centuries have blurred the tribal boundaries. At local level, in fact, they were probably never maintained very well. If the purpose of discrimination was to concentrate property in the hands of Protestants, then the Catholic who managed to hold on to his property had, so to speak, beaten the game. Social contact was maintained between the better Catholic families and the Protestant gentry, and marriage across the tribal boundary was not uncommon.

All this interchange has meant that it is impossible to distinguish any purely Protestant racial stock. O'Briens, MacNamaras, Butlers, Plunketts have had branches in both religions for centuries. The same name is no proof of the same racial origins: Jennings, for instance, is an anglicised form of Mac Seóinín, a branch of the Burkes of Connacht; but it is a common English name too and must have been borne by many settlers.[14] Two Grays appear side by side in the deaths column of the same newspaper on the same day. Both are from Cavan. One can distinguish the Catholic from the Methodist by the letters RIP.

There is a 95 per cent chance that any citizen of the Republic, picked at random, will be (at least for census purposes) a Catholic. There are thousands more Murphys, Kellys, Byrnes, O'Briens, O'Neills, O'Connors, O'Sullivans, McCarthys in the Catholic tribe than in the Protestant. A Pim, perhaps, would sound like a Protestant. So (to a Corkman) would a Daunt or a Kingston. A White is perfectly indistinguishable. But a list of names can create a pattern which *must* be Protestant, especially if Christian names and surnames are taken together. Here for instance is the senior class in a school :

Beamish, Rosemary
Beamish, Sam

Bryan, Eleanor
Clarke, Eva

Coombes, Ann
Culbert, Henry
Giles, Jennifer
Jagoe, Joy
Lovell, Hilary
McCutcheon, Elizabeth

Perrott, Sandra
Roycroft, Hazel
Schiller, Karen
Shorten, Ruth
Smith, Victor
Webb, Gertrude.

Not a single Irish name—no Seán, no Máire. Not a single familiar saint. Take the list as a whole and it might hail from Shropshire. The skilled eye will identify it at once as Protestant. Indeed, on the evidence of a few names (Beamish, Coombes, Roycroft) it can almost be assigned to a particular district : the full school roll would produce others (Swanton, Kingston, Hosford, Vickery) which together give it an unmistakable flavour of West Cork. Most of these families are solid Protestant farmers whose roots go back perhaps three or four centuries—in the same area, in the same district, almost on the same land. During all this time, as a small minority surrounded by a vast majority of Catholics, they have kept a kind of cultural identity which is summed up in the pattern of their names. By now it is questionable whether that identity can survive more than another couple of generations.

4

The Lost Victory

T H E R E is no way of defining a minority except by reference to a majority. One of the themes of modern Irish history has been this question : where does majority end and minority began? In Northern Ireland there is a confrontation of two minorities : the Catholics a minority in the Six Counties, the Protestants a minority in all Ireland. But the Protestant sees himself, at the same time, as a member of a larger majority, the stable Protestant majority of the United Kingdom. By the end of the eighteenth century it was becoming clear that Irish Protestants could not maintain a position of privilege indefinitely against the demands of a huge and growing Catholic majority. The Union in 1800 offered the promise that, when Catholics finally gained political power in Ireland, they would be held in check by the weight of the Protestant majority in the United Kingdom. It became a fundamental objective of Protestant policy to maintain this position.

The Union lasted for 120 years, but it had not run much more than half its course when the positions which it was designed to defend were all but overrun. For the final fifty years of its history the Garrison was merely holding out under siege. The census of 1861 showed how the forces were balanced. Catholics made up nearly 78 per cent of a population of 5,800,000. Within a few years Gladstone had disestablished the Church of Ireland. Before very much longer the land laws were to divide up the big estates and break the power of the landlords. The balance of parliamentary representation was shifting, under the influence of the secret ballot, towards men who were middle-class in origin, Catholic in religion, nationalist in politics. Home Rule, the unthinkable disaster, was presented to parliament in 1886 and again in 1893. Local government was in the hands of the majority from 1898 onwards. It must have been difficult for any partisan of Protestant Ascendancy not to see the writing on the wall.

For the political historian the dominating figure in the earlier part of the century is that of Daniel O'Connell. By securing Catholic Emancipation he gave the Catholic a licence, for the first time, to compete on equal terms with the Protestant. He failed, it is true, in the second stage of his great campaign—to secure the repeal of the Union itself. The English political machine was not yet ready to go into reverse. But he succeeded in mobilising the mass of Catholic opinion. He brought the poor into politics by way of subscriptions of a penny a month to his campaign fund; he brought the clergy into politics as an essential element in his organisation; he brought the Catholic Church into politics, so that in the latter part of the century it functioned as a kind of party above parties. It was the church party, essentially, which fought for and won disestablishment, denominational education, and eventually a system of higher education acceptable to Catholics. From the mid-century onwards the bishops had no hesitation in speaking as the voice of the Irish people. O'Connell not only made Catholics effective, he made them *feel* effective : he made them aware of their own strength.

O'Connell, then, won only one battle, but it was a vital battle; and he left the army behind him, mobilised and trained for others to use. It was of course a Catholic army; and this, in a larger sense, was its limitation. The success of O'Connell meant that the vision of '98, the vision of Tone—'to unite the whole people of Ireland, to abolish the memory of all past dissensions, and to substitute the common name of Irishman in place of the denominations of Catholic, Protestant and Dissenter' —would never again be within grasp.

Tone's objective had been to overthrow the Protestant Ascendancy and break the connection with England. His method was to work for an alliance between the oppressed Catholics and the Presbyterians of the North. The Presbyterians were the mainspring of the entire mechanism, and it is worth quoting his assessment of them.

The Dissenters are, from the genius of their religion and the spirit of inquiry which it produces, sincere and enlightened republicans; they have ever, in a degree, opposed the usurpation of England. . . . Still, however, in all the civil wars of Ireland they ranged themselves under the standard of England, and were the most formidable enemies to the Catholic natives, whom they detested as Papists, and despised as slaves. . . . [Under the influence of the French Revolution] they saw that, whilst they thought they were the masters of the Catholics, they were, in fact, but their jailers, and that, instead of enjoying liberty in their own country, they served but as a garrison to keep it in subjection to England. . . . Catholics and Dissenters, the two great sects whose mutual animosities have been the radical weakness of their country, are at length reconciled, and the arms which have been so often imbrued in the blood of each other are ready for the first time to be turned in concert against the common enemy.[1]

What, after all, became of this alliance? How did the republicans of one generation become the loyalists of the next? To some extent, perhaps, Tone was creating his own myth. Support for the United Irishmen was always strongest in those parts of Ulster where Catholics were thin on the ground. 'Those Protestants who hated the Catholic more than the landlord became Orangemen,' writes a Presbyterian historian, 'while those who hated the landlord more than the Catholic became United Irishmen.'[2] All along, perhaps, their revolutionary principles had grown less from reason than from resentment—resentment against the landlord, resentment against the Established Church, resentment built up over a century of calculated discrimination. When the rising broke out in Wexford, and word came through of the outrages against Protestants, 'Presbyterians began to think it better to bear the oppression of the rectors and the landlords than to be piked by Papists'. With the threat of a new terror before them, all the fears of 1641 were revived, and their impulse was to seek for Protestant solidarity against the old enemy.

O'Connell's success presented the threat in a new form: a threat to privilege rather than to lives and property. At the same time Anglican and Dissenter were swept closer together by the rising tide of the evangelical movement. It was at this critical point that Henry Cooke became the dominant figure of Northern Presbyterianism. Cooke, a preacher and orator of exceptional talent, became the champion of old-style orthodoxy in religion and old-style Toryism in politics, against the more liberal principles of the 'New Light' party. He won control of the Presbyterian General Assembly, and he used the organised force of Presbyterianism effectively to end the lingering forms of discrimination (Presbyterian marriages were not fully legalised until 1844) and to mould the new national school system to his own demands. But he also placed Presbyterian opinion firmly behind the Conservative Party. By the mid-century, Dissent had become Assent—in political terms at least. In 1912 the descendants of the United Irishmen were taking up arms, with the blessing of their ministers, to fight against Home Rule.

* * *

For the mass of people in the countryside the Union signified very little. Although the two kingdoms were united, and a single parliament sat at Westminster, there remained a separate administration in Dublin Castle; and that administration was dominated still by the Protestant Ascendancy. At local level the landlord and the parson remained the natural enemies of the peasantry. Of the two, perhaps the parson was the more resented. Catholic tenants, already overburdened with rent, bitterly objected to the additional imposition of tithes paid to support the clergy of an heretical church. During the 1830s a campaign was launched, marked by violence and intimidation, to stop the payment of tithes. In the last resort, of course, the church could appeal to the state to enforce its legal rights. In 1834 Archdeacon Ryder of Gortroe, Co. Cork, who was Justice of the Peace as well as rector of the parish, led out a force of horse, foot and police to secure payment of forty shillings in tithes from a Widow Ryan. The widow's neighbours rallied to defend her home with sticks and pitchforks; the soldiers used swords and bayonets, and eventually opened fire; and by the time they retired the archdeacon's army left twelve of the local people dead and forty-two wounded on the battlefield. This shocking affray, and others like it, showed up the urgent need for a reform of the law. By an act of 1838 tithes were attached to rent, and the obligation of payment laid on the landlord. It was, of course, a compromise which did not touch the objectionable principle of tithe-payment, but it served to remove the immediate grievance.

Meanwhile the whole of rural Ireland was moving inexorably towards a disaster which would dwarf all other disasters in its history. The moving force was a population explosion of astonishing proportions, which pushed the population of the island up from about five millions in 1800 to around 6·8 millions twenty years later, and over eight millions by the 1840s. Whatever the explanation, this vast increase—occurring mainly among the poorest agricultural classes—forced the standard of living of the peasantry down to the lowest level of miserable subsistence. Only the potato kept them fed at all. When the potato failed during the 1840s, famine was inevitable.

* * *

There were people who saw the Famine as a divine visitation. 'Since the Famine in 1846,' wrote one of them, 'the minds of the people have been gradually prepared for the reception of the faithful and affectionate preaching of the Gospel.'[3] These were the evangelical preachers, who reached the highest point of their activity in Ireland during the black 1840s. The evangelical movement represents the first real burst of missionary activity in the history of the Irish Church; and objective estimate is made difficult by the fact that it coincided with the most terrible period of suffering in recorded Irish history. The preachers themselves saw the coincidence as the will of God: the Rev. Alexander Dallas noted that 'the awful famine of 1847, with its attendant horrors in 1848, worked wonderfully' for the movement. But in Irish popular tradition the preachers survive only as 'soupers'— unscrupulous peddlers in souls, who used pots of broth and bags of meal as bribes to induce the starving people to abandon their faith.

We can find the origins of the movement not in Ireland but in England, with the rise of the evangelical party in the English Church.

They were men not of theory but of practice, content to base their activities on an uncompromising affirmation of their faith in the fundamental principle of Protestant religion. This Protestant belief brought them close to the Dissenters;

and in 1846 they founded the Evangelical Alliance, which, though not without friction from both sides, united all English Protestants, Churchmen and Nonconformists, in a common hatred of Roman Catholicism, and of every Catholic influence in the Church of England.[4]

For anyone who wanted to combat Rome, Ireland offered a ready battlefield. The work in Ireland had begun with the Bible societies, which used the Bible in Irish as a textbook for elementary education. The missionaries were well supported with funds, and they soon found it convenient—to ward off intimidation and prevent backsliding—to gather their converts into colonies. Charles Gayer set up a colony at Dingle, Edward Nangle a more celebrated settlement on Achill Island (some of the buildings still survive), while Alexander Dallas and the Irish Church Missions carried on the campaign on a wide front in the West.

This wave of evangelical zeal claimed at its height many thousands of converts; yet it subsided leaving hardly a trace behind—hardly a trace, that is, but the bitter belief, indelibly etched in the Irish folk-memory, that the missionaries came to buy souls for soup.

> The proselytiser, ever seeing in these periods of distress the dispensing hand of Providence, charitably undertook to fill the mouth of the starving Papist, only asking in return that he would consent to make acquaintance with the Protestant Bible.[5]

The phrase is revealing. No missioner would have conceived of a 'Protestant Bible'. To them the Bible was unique and universal, the Word of God, the rightful inheritance of every man with a soul to be saved; and any power which restricted the access of the people to the Word must be adjudged corrupt and unholy. The spiritual starvation of the people seemed to them a much greater deprivation than their physical starvation. Dallas himself, referring to the extreme distress of the poor, noted that 'the principal evil arising from it might be, that it would induce starving creatures to make a false profession of conversion, for the sake of being brought into notice, and perhaps obtaining relief'. Dr Desmond Bowen is surely right when he attributes some of the success of the missions to 'the awful depression of spirit' that came over the country folk during the period :

> For many Irish people the famine years were a time of religious crisis, and their agony was spiritual as well as physical. A deep and abiding gloom descended upon them, and when Scripture Readers spoke of the famine as a divine visitation for national sin many listened.[6]

We may be unjust and unimaginative if we paint a sordid picture of a bribe being offered on the one hand, and accepted on the other. The missioners—fearsome as their zeal may appear in retrospect—were meeting what they believed to be the deepest need of the people. As for those who 'jumped', they may have needed more than food : they may have needed help to remake the structure of their universe.

Among the resident clergy of the Church of Ireland there were many who disapproved of the missions, believing that they could be productive of nothing but sectarian strife. On the other hand a contemporary speaks of the 'affection and respect' with which Dallas was greeted on his travels in the West: 'Wherever Mr Dallas went he was received with the *céad míle fáilte*, bonfires and hearty cheers.'[7] And the record, if it can be trusted, is remarkable. At Clifden, a region with scarcely a single 'original Protestant', there were 1,800 children on the school roll in 1850. More than a thousand persons passed the examination of the visiting inspector in Irish. In October 1849 the Bishop of Tuam confirmed 401 converts. But a later clerical visitor at a mission centre in Roscommon reported that, of eighty persons associated with the mission, seventy-one had emigrated in three years, 'being obliged to seek in a strange country the means of subsistence which bigotry and persecution on the one side, and deficiency of funds on the other, prevented their obtaining in their native land'.[8] And this seems to have been, in the long run, the fate of the missions. Those who were firm in their new faith were obliged to emigrate in order to find freedom to practise it. Those who remained, 'having endured persecution for a time, fell away and went back to their former errors and superstitions'. The missionary accounts suggest that hostility was rarely spontaneous—it was generated by the Catholic priests— but we must recognise that in this matter the witnesses are very partial. Nevertheless, if the missions did nothing else they obliged the Catholic Church to throw a new effort into desolate regions which had been starved of pastoral care.

In the North, the evangelical flame was kept burning brightly by the remarkable religious revival of 1859, and a closer understanding and solidarity developed between Anglican and Dissenter as a result of their work in the mission field. In the Church of Ireland itself, the evangelical spirit survived, to play a central part in the reshaping of both the structures and the observances of the church after disestablishment.

* * *

One of the districts most ravaged by the Famine was the area of West Cork from Skibbereen to the Mizen Head. The rector of The Altar, William A. Fisher, had been there only a few years when the blight came. Fisher was an Englishman, and he seems to have had no previous connection with Ireland when he was posted to this poor and remote parish. He set to work at once to learn Irish, and constantly stopped, on his rounds of the parish, to chat to the people he met on the roads. His regular Sunday ministrations began with a service at the Mizen Head, followed by one at Crookhaven; on to Sunday-school at Goleen, and then to evening service at Caha. All told a day like this must have meant some six to eight hours in the saddle.

When the Famine came he spent all his time and energy on relief work, setting up soup kitchens and distributing the food himself for hours at a time, then setting off on horseback to visit the fever-stricken people in their cottages with food and medicines. He built the church known as Teampall na mBocht as a relief work, adding money of his own to the funds available. Some of those he visited tried, in the throes of fever or hunger, to make their confession to him. From one of his sayings we may judge that he would have been an understanding confessor: 'Never compare sins. One is as great an offence against God as another: only he knows the differences of character and situation by which to weigh them.'

Fisher spent forty years in this parish—from 1840 to 1880—and seems to have been regarded with respect and affection. In his last years, 1879–80, the area was again stricken by famine, and the rector's house was besieged by wretched people looking for food. He gave out bags of meal, with the strict injunction that the people must not neglect to cultivate their land and sow their crops, and he wrote desperately to all possible donors for more relief. His own parishioners were not much better off than their Catholic neighbours : there were, he reported, forty men in the parish who could not come to church because they had nothing to wear, and thirty more who had to exchange clothes with their sons so that each might attend in turn. A woman told him that the clothing of her four daughters 'would not be enough to clean a candlestick'. When other donors failed him he pledged his own credit, to the extent of £60, to secure bags of meal from the merchant 'for families that I know, and know well, had not a bit to put in their mouths. . . . If the crop is good I have no doubt but that the poor fellows will pay it with gratitude by their labour, but if not I purpose to pay for it out of my stipend when the half-year is up.'

From all this we get a picture of an old-fashioned pastoral clergyman who regarded all the people of the parish—not only those who came to his communion table—as being in some sense under his charge.

> He was accustomed to speak of those whose views differed from his own, if he believed them to be pious men, as seeing *another side* of truth. He used to say that she was many-sided, and that each person could only see one part; so that if there were no differences of opinion nothing would be truly known, as one part is the complement of another.[9]

Fisher's form of Christianity was evidently very different from the Christianity of Dallas or Nangle; or of the Rev. Charles Seymour, of Tuam, who held the gates of the Catholic cathedral closed by force, to prevent the passage of the Corpus Christi procession, as a protest against the 'idolatrous ceremony'. Both are, in their own way, typical enough of their period, and elements of both traditions still permeated the disestablished church at the end of the nineteenth century.

* * *

The Act of Union in 1800 not only brought about a union between the parliaments of England and Ireland : it also effected a union between the Church of England and the Church of Ireland. The preservation of this united church 'was to be deemed and taken to be an essential and fundamental part of

the Union'. In fact the Union was less than seventy years old
when this part of its foundation was cut away by the disestablishment of the Church of Ireland. Disestablishment was
the achievement of the Catholic Church in Ireland, functioning
as a political body, in alliance with the English Liberal Nonconformists. It was an odd alliance, because the two parties were
at odds on the basic principle of church-state relations. The
English Nonconformists were inspired by Garibaldi, who had
undertaken to break the hold of the Pope on church lands in
Italy. The Irish Catholic bishops were ardent supporters of
papal rights. In the words of a leading authority,

> They [the bishops] were working for the establishment in
> Ireland of the very principles over which Pius IX had joined
> issue with the Italian Liberals in his excruciating endeavour
> to preserve the connexion of Church and State and prevent
> the secularisation of ecclesiastical property. The Irish bishops
> therefore flew in the face of the *Syllabus of Errors* in a cam-
> paign to attain that which the Papacy most dreaded : 'a free
> church in a free state.' In this way also they used their
> influence to endorse the changing view of the state, from the
> protector of exclusive religious beliefs to a neutral arbiter
> between competing religious opinions, in the most effective
> way they could. Or to put it differently, they worked for the
> attainment of a Liberal State.[10]

In strict logic the bishops should perhaps have pressed for the
endowment of the Catholic Church as a state church. In fact
there was a lobby for the principle of 'concurrent endowment',
by which they meant the division of the church revenues
between all denominations in proportion to their numbers.
However, the bishops threw their weight in favour of total
separation of church from state, with no endowment by the
state of any religion; and this principle, embodied in Gladstone's
act of 1869, has governed church-state relations in Ireland
down to the present day.

Disestablishment was resisted to the hilt by the Church of
Ireland : it was denounced as impiety, as pillage, as destruction.
Now, after a lapse of a hundred years, it would be hard to find
anybody, layman or cleric, who will not acknowledge that it
was a real and a necessary reform. In the event, the achieve-

ment of disestablishment was much more than a restructuring—however drastic—of church finances. It superimposed a system of democratic control upon a hierarchical body. It brought laymen into the government of the church at every level, from the parish to the national General Synod. It produced an episcopal church with a constitution no less democratic, in practice, than those of the Nonconformist churches. It turned a religious institution into a religious community.

Little of this prospect was discerned by the Church of Ireland bishops. They seem to have had a vision that the godly people of England would arise in their wrath and smite down William Ewart Gladstone. In fact the British electorate accepted the proposals with considerable equanimity, and even the Tories made a pretty half-hearted defence. Disraeli appeared to argue that a state church was needed as a sort of refuge for the destitute, like a spiritual workhouse. Those who argued that the church was being despoiled had their guns well spiked by Sir John Gray, who pointed out how much the ecclesiastics had done to purloin church property in the interests of their own families. The Primate, Marcus Beresford, headed the list: he and his relatives held upwards of seven thousand acres of church land at just over 4s. an acre, something like one-tenth of its normal value. In all Sir John reckoned that in just over thirty years Irish landlords had pocketed some £4,250,000 in tithe rents which were intended for the church.

The first effect of the Irish Church Act was to sever the connection between church and state. The property of the church, with the exception of churches and graveyards actually in use, was confiscated, and vested in a body of commissioners. The commissioners were to make provision to pay each of the existing clergy for life. At the same time the state payment to Presbyterian ministers (the *regium donum*) and the annual grant to the Catholic Maynooth College were to be cut off, compensation being paid for both interests out of church property. Glebe lands and houses were to be sold back to the church at a low valuation.

The Church of Ireland responded to disestablishment with unexpected resilience. The clergy themselves, by commuting their life-interests, created a new endowment; the Representative Church Body, set up to administer the temporal affairs of the church, was able to invest this new capital in such a way as to pay their annuities and provide a surplus for other purposes. At the same time a Church Convention was summoned to create a new constitution for the church. Government now passed into the hands of elected assemblies with substantial lay representation at parochial, diocesan and national level.

Disestablishment did undoubtedly cause many Irish Protestants to feel that they had been cut off and abandoned by a trusted guardian. They were disappointed and bitter at the cold indifference with which the English Anglicans regarded their fate. Politically, the effect was to confirm their support of the Conservative Party against a Liberal Party which had sold them down the river. When Gladstone entered on the next stage of the great betrayal, with the First Home Rule Bill of 1886, a special General Synod was held to oppose it. When the Second Home Rule Bill was introduced, Dr H. Kingsmill Moore, who organised the protest campaign, recorded that not a single vestry in Ireland refused to support the protest, and throughout the thirteen dioceses there were only forty-one dissenting votes.[11]

It is clear, all the same, that even if they had been successful in holding back disestablishment, they could not have held back independence; and independence and establishment could not be compatible. If Gladstone's act had been fought off for another fifty years, then the severance of church and state would have taken place in 1920; and it is hard to see how it could have been accomplished then without a disruption of the church itself. In the event the Church of Ireland survived into a divided Ireland as an undivided body.

5
The Twilight of Ascendancy

Irish Protestantism was not then a religion: it was a side
in political faction, a class prejudice, a conviction that Roman
Catholics are socially inferior persons who will go to Hell
when they die and leave Heaven in the exclusive possession
of Protestant ladies and gentlemen.[1]

GEORGE BERNARD SHAW (1898)

THE Diamond Jubilee of Her Gracious Majesty Queen
Victoria in June 1897 was marked in Dublin by appropriate
celebrations. The morning found the city wearing a festive and
picturesque appearance. Union Jacks flew from the principal
buildings, including the Bank of Ireland, Trinity College and
Guinness's Brewery. Services of thanksgiving were held in St
Patrick's Cathedral and local churches. Tasteful decorations
were displayed by leading business houses, and Sackville Street
never looked brighter with bunting and illuminations.

This was the observation of the *Irish Times*, which also
reported on the celebrations in Simla, Madras and Hyderabad,
Cape Town, Sydney, Ballarat and Penang. In its leading article
the paper was concerned to strike a note of harmony. The spirit
of the festival, it said, was in no way political:

It is not in any way a triumph of any portion of the Queen's
subjects over another. It is not a declaration of any policy
beyond that of Imperial unity.[2]

The Dublin *Daily Express* was less restrained:

The grand fact, which needed no celebration to engrave itself
deeply on every British heart, is that Victoria has reigned
for sixty years, that those sixty years have been in every

c

way the most prominent, and the most prosperous in the history of our country. . . . We have acquired, a glorious Empire: we are prepared to keep it.[3]

On the evening of the festival Trinity College students burst out into the streets, armed with sticks and chanting 'God Save the Queen', to break up an anti-jubilee demonstration which was organised by the Irish Socialist Republican League and addressed by Mr James Connolly and Miss Maud Gonne. In the morning, no doubt, the children of the Model Schools marched out as O'Casey describes them marching on the King's birthday:

> The gathering of children headed by Slogan the schoolmaster and Hunter the minister, moving off on their way to witness the review. Each child wore a red-white-and-blue rosette and oul' Slogan carried a small Union Jack.[4]

Both groups represented Protestant youth, though on different rungs of the social ladder. Both turned out to demonstrate not simply loyalty, but that sense of identity which warmed the British heart of the *Express*.

* * *

The Irish society of a century earlier had been a colonial society, but it had felt the impulse of its own heartbeat, and it had been prepared to consider cutting the umbilical cord. The society which celebrated Victoria's jubilee was the product of almost a century of Union; its bloodstream was linked to the heartbeat of Mother England. The symbolic focus of attachment was the Crown, and the reflected glory of royalty bathed the Lord Lieutenant and his lady. A children's fancy-dress ball at the viceregal lodge merited a report in a 'society journal':

> The little guests were of course the children of the upper crust of Dublin Society. . . . There can be no doubt that on the costumes provided for the occasion a good deal of money must have been spent, giving employment to a considerable number of young girls in city *modistes'* establishments.[5]

Like the Court, much of Dublin's high-life was second-hand: anything from gowns to operettas came by way of London. The columnists did their best to help the Hibernian metropolis to keep pace:

The 'banjo fad' is the strongest craze of Society at present. Since it was mooted that the Prince of Wales was acquiring a knowledge and manipulation of this instrument all sorts and conditions of society have followed his example.[6]

Shaw, looking back on his youth, savaged this provincial pantomime:

To an outsider there is nothing but comedy in the spectacle of a forlorn set of Protestant merchants in a Catholic country, led by a petty plutocracy of stockbrokers, doctors and land-agents, and camouflaged by that section of the landed gentry who, too heavily mortgaged to escape to London, play at being a Court and an aristocracy. . . . To such pretences, involving continual lying as to income and social standing, were sacrificed all the realities of life.[7]

Upper class parents thought it right to beggar themselves, if necessary, to send their sons to English public schools, where they might acquire the outlook, the manners, and above all the accent of the English gentleman. Many of the boys went on to make careers in the army or the colonial service. If they returned at last to Ireland, they had a habit of bringing home English wives. In ways like these the Protestant upper classes maintained a network of intimate bonds with their own class in Britain and throughout the Empire.

* * *

'The world whose beginnings Dickens had celebrated stuck somehow here, its growth arrested.' So L. A. G. Strong describes the Dublin he knew about the turn of the century.

In a provincial, decadent form this era lasted on in Dublin well into the early nineteen hundreds. It was maintained by a class numerically and spiritually narrow, a tiny blackcoated incubus, a ruling caste: the Protestant well-to-do, in whose hands was vested all influence, all authority, all patronage: a class so deeply, so instinctively prejudiced that Grandpapa, the most charitable of men, who would pick up a worm from the path for fear it should be trodden, cried out indignantly if a strange Catholic approached his door. Yet his cook, his gardener, all his servants were Catholics. He treated them with the utmost consideration and kindness, and they bore him no ill-will for his opinions, which they found as much a fact as the facts of wealth and poverty, birth and humble living.[8]

The student of colonial societies will have no difficulty in recognising the picture. In Ireland the contours are sometimes hard to follow because the map is three-dimensional: creed, class and political allegiance fall together in patterns always recognisable but not always regular. There were poor Protestants as well as poor Catholics, though not so many. There were rich Catholics as well as rich Protestants. At a certain level birth or income outweighed religious distinctions, and the Catholic who was noble or rich became a kind of honorary Protestant. Still, the keys of the door remained firmly in the hands of the minority. Dublin had seen relatively little industrial development of the kind that creates new concentrations of wealth, and hence of power and prestige. The major manufacturing concerns, like Guinness's and Jacob's, were traditionally Protestant, and smaller-scale business had no claim to social distinction. In a comment scribbled on a manuscript by his cousin Charles, Bernard Shaw wrote:

> It was simply the rule in Dublin that, though business had to be admitted as gentlemanly, it must be wholesale business. Keeping a shop was unpardonable. Lucy [his sister] was troubled all her life by the guilty secret that our father's mill at Dolphin's Barn had a little village shop attached to it.[9]

In the professions Catholics had advanced rapidly during the latter part of the nineteenth century, but in the upper reaches and where patronage counted—among judges and senior counsel, for instance—Protestants had an overwhelming majority. In the bank service they outnumbered Catholics by more than two to one. In the civil service numbers began to approach equality in the decade before the Great War, but the only grade in which the religious majority held a majority of jobs was at the lowly level of messenger. The creation of the National University established a second (and Catholic) academic world alongside the Protestant world of Trinity, but Trinity retained its social primacy. In 1915 a professor of the National University wrote:

I have only once in my life dined in a Protestant house. I have never drunk afternoon tea in the drawingroom of a member of the late Established Church. . . . Years ago, by an accident, I once found myself at a charity ball organised by Protestants of the upper middle class for some non-sectarian purpose. I found that the only girl I knew in the room was the only Catholic.[10]

* * *

> Sing the peasantry, and then
> Hard-riding country gentlemen . . .

Yeats was not the man to sing the bespoke bootmaker and the corporation clerk; and because there was nobody to sing them they have been largely forgotten. There were 50,000 Protestants in the Dublin of 1901, and of these only a tiny fraction could ever have been involved with what the journals called 'society'. Few, perhaps, knew the conditions of grinding poverty that O'Casey describes as the background of his own youth; but among the little streets off the North Strand or the South Circular Road there were thousands of Protestant families on the lower fringe of the middle class. A writer who was brought up in this world recalls that among his neighbours—in Fontenoy Street, behind the Black Church—Protestant families numbered about one in three: 'Differences of religion were rarely mentioned in those days, and I have the happiest recollection of the kindness and goodwill of our Catholic neighbours and friends.'[11]

For this family the great event of the year was an outing in a hired landau to the annual military review in the Phoenix Park. At the Presbyterian school in Hardwicke Street—which mustered about a hundred pupils—the classroom 'was decorated with pictures of royalty and representatives of British military prowess, as indeed were many homes, Protestant and Catholic alike'. History was taught from *Little Arthur's History of England*, and at the end of the Boer War the children sported buttons with the pictures of the British war-heroes, Roberts and Baden-Powell. Patriotism, in this sense, was the common—indeed the obligatory—attitude of their religious and social group. As a fellow-student exclaims, scandalised, to George A. Birmingham's *Hyacinth*,

Good Lord! You don't mean to tell me that you are a pro-Boer, and you a Divinity student![12]

* * *

'Between about 1890 and 1910 Ireland appeared, outwardly at least, to have become a more prosperous, more contented, more somnolent country.'[13] Certainly this was the view from the Big House; and in some respects the appearance was not very far from the reality. In *The Real Charlotte*, the finest of their works, Somerville and Ross show us a world untouched by any premonition of change. Here is the social tapestry of a country town in the 1890s: the landlord, the agent, the parson, the officers in garrison, and all their ladies hovering about them. At the top, unchallenged, are Lord and Lady Dysart; the standing of everyone else is measured by his or her distance from the Dysarts. But the world of Lismoyle is a curious world, because it is a world of Protestants. Even Francie, the enchanting vulgarian, is impeccably Anglican, her social life centred on Sunday-school and choir practice. Catholics in Lismoyle are servants and fishwomen.[14]

By the 1890s, of course, this picture of a country town was already out of date. The Protestant middle class maintained its conviction of social superiority, but it had little enough to feel superior about. The new Catholic middle class outweighed it in numbers and rivalled it in wealth: the outward and visible sign was the lavish expenditure on churches, convents and the like. Local government had been placed in the hands of elected councils, which reflected the outlook of the majority—or, perhaps more accurately, of its local leaders. The power of patronage moved from the landlords and the big businessmen to these new men. Still, however, the Protestant gentry remained quietly confident that the country could not get on without them. 'Our class,' says an old gentleman in a novel of the 1900s, 'alone of all the people in this distracted country, has any conception of the meaning of the word citizenship.'[15]

In the event, as the statistics show, the Protestant population of the country towns melted away much faster than in the surrounding countryside. Part of the reason, perhaps, is that so many of the leaders of this society were essentially transients. The officers, of course, were recognised as birds of passage; but a great many others—bank managers, government inspectors, railway officials, even the ministers of religion—were outsiders, careerists, liable to move on to other posts, or at least to retire to Greystones or Kingstown and leave not a trace behind. Even their social activities—bridge circles or dramatic societies— often depended on the initiative of one person and collapsed when he or she moved on. This may be why they had so little sticking power, why they failed to produce any leadership which might have been more representative than that of the land-owners. They had no roots, and they made none.

* * *

The leaders to whom the Protestants now committed their fortunes were drawn, in the main, from the group of men least equipped to display a flexible understanding of the aspirations of a new Ireland: the large landowners. Their spokesman at the turn of the century, Colonel E. J. Saunderson, was an extraordinary combination of sporting squire and pulpit-thumper. Projecting an attack on Parnell and the First Home Rule Bill, he wrote to his wife:

> I feel confident that God is with me, and that He will give me the stone of David which will bring the giant crashing to the ground.[16]

After 1910, when it was evident that the Ulstermen were going their own way, the leader selected by Southern Unionists was the Earl of Midleton, a nobleman of English birth and educa-tion, whose only connection with Ireland was that he happened to have large estates in Co. Cork. The political movement which he led, although no doubt it commanded the electoral support of the great majority of Southern Protestants, was basically designed to protect the interests of the propertied class.

Not surprisingly, the leaders of Unionism were anxious to rebut the notion that it represented only the landed gentry. A pamphlet of 1886 protested:

> Many persons outside Ireland confound the Loyalists with the Landlords. . . . The Landlords form a comparatively small section of the Loyal party in Ireland; they are in fact no more the Loyalists of Ireland than the Parnellites are the Irish people. . . . This loyalty exists among the professional and mercantile classes quite as strongly as among the land-lords; and even among the farming class . . . there are large

numbers who are sincerely desirous to preserve the union between the two countries.[17]

Nor, it added, was loyalty the monopoly of Protestants:

> There are large numbers of Roman Catholics, both lay and clerical, who are as firmly attached to the British connection as the most devotedly loyal Protestant in the land.

These protestations do not much affect our estimate of the character of the movement. The Home Rule movement had begun, after the introduction of the Ballot Act in 1872, to bring the middle classes into active politics: men like Joe Biggar, a provision merchant from Belfast, brought a common touch into parliament, and with it a new streak of toughness. No such broadening took place within Unionism. 'Now and then', wrote Horace Plunkett, 'an individual tries to broaden the base of Irish Unionism, and to bring himself into touch with the life of the people; but the nearer he gets to the people the farther he gets from the Irish Unionist leaders.'[18]

The businessmen had rather more flexibility of mind than the landowners. They were afraid, to be sure, that if Home Rule came they might be ruined by incompetent or even malicious administration. But they were aware that it was not Protestants who ate most of the flour, drank most of the porter, or smoked most of the plug tobacco. A recent study of Unionism in Cork—where there was an exceptionally strong mercantile class—makes the distinction clearly:

> Commercial or city Unionism was suspect: its greater integration, and its lesser economic friction with groups around it, meant that defections could, and did, take place more frequently from its ranks. Only in landed Unionism was there a strong élitist conception, an unique economic position, and an important imperial tradition.[19]

A Dublin businessman put it in plain terms: 'You should recollect that we businessmen in Dublin live by the nationalists in the country towns, and there is no use in *abusing* them.'[20]

For the ordinary Protestant of the rank and file, however, the argument was irrelevant. He had no property to defend. He had far more in common—so one might think—with the Catholic of the same class than with the gentry. Yet he was persuaded to regard Home Rule as a calamity, and to throw his support behind the landlords in the effort to preserve the Union.

* * *

Why did these ordinary lower-middle-class Protestants support the interests of their socially superior co-religionists?

Habit comes into it. The gentry were accustomed to be leaders; the clerks and the small farmers were accustomed to be led. In church itself, the brazen militarism of Victorian hymns—'Like a mighty army, Moves the Church of God'— had bred in them a vision of the Soldiers of Christ moving together, shoulder to shoulder, against the heathen and the ungodly. The gentry were the officer class: they commanded on the battlefield, they occupied the front pews in church, they were elected to the vestries and synods. The humbler Protestants knew their place. They were too docile to suggest—if it ever occurred to them—that influence should not necessarily be equated with property.

Furthermore, they had, or thought they had, some share of privilege themselves. Their share of the good jobs was out of all proportion to their numbers, and the challenge to their privileged position was becoming more and more vocal as the middle-class Catholics increased in numbers and self-confidence. In 1908 the *New Ireland Review* pointed to blatant discrimination in the distribution of senior posts in the Bank of Ireland. 'More and more of real power is certain to pass before long into the hands of the Catholic majority,' the journal commented. 'How will the majority use it? Not, we trust, in a sectarian spirit. . . . But of one thing we may be assured; they will see that justice is done to Catholics.'[21]

Protestants tended to believe that 'justice' for Catholics in a Home Rule Ireland would mean a monopoly; and no doubt there were some Catholics who had the same idea. A lecturer before the Catholic Commercial Club in 1900 put forward the celebrated theory of 'other things being equal':

Even in the material concerns of life, we Catholics should give special and preferential aid to each other. In our friendships, in our social relations, in our professional and business deal-ings, our common Faith should not be disregarded. Other things being equal, it should be a determining element in our decisions. It should even, it seems to me, outweigh, within a measure, some temporal advantages.[22]

This attempt to put a moral gloss on jobbery would have been repudiated by many Irishmen of the time. Nevertheless it sums up the fears of many Irish Protestants. They did not fear a pogrom; but they did fear the pressure of a majority, backed by the absolute authority of the Catholic Church. They feared for the whole Protestant community what T. W. Russell feared for Ulster:

The whole thing means that if you set up a Parliament on College Green, the wealth, education, property and prosperity of Ulster will be handed over to a Parliament which will be elected by peasants dominated by priests, and they again will be dominated by the Roman Catholic Church.[23]

Home Rule, in the well-known phrase, would turn out to be Rome Rule.

* * *

The ordinary Protestants backed their leaders because, in the last resort, a Protestant clerk felt closer to a Protestant gentleman than to a Catholic clerk. He felt closer because he shared with the gentleman two basic differences from all their Catholic fellow-citizens: a different concept of religion, and a different concept of nationality.

Deep in the fabric of all Protestants there is a belief in the importance of the Reformation as one of the great liberations of human history. They believe in it as a bursting of the bars, as a triumph of the spirit of the individual over the dead hand of the institution. They believe that, through Luther's protest, the individual asserted his right to direct communion with God, and that he derived his authority from the scriptures. His church leaders had no higher authority than this, to which he himself had equal access. The Protestant sees his church as an institution created to serve him in his religious life. In the great debate on disestablishment the argument centred on property— the spoliation of the church, the right of the state to alienate church property, the danger to all other property if the precedent were admitted. But it was never suggested that an established church was necessary as a tent-pole for Protestantism. Protestants would have been just as surely Protestant if there had been no church at all.

They saw the Church of Rome, by contrast, as a vast monolithic institution which demanded total obedience from all its adherents. Not very many Irish Protestants seriously believed that their destinies were going to be governed from the Vatican. But they had been raised in homes where *Foxe's Book of Martyrs* stood in the bookcase; they held, printed on childhood memory, the vivid picture of the brave Protestant at the stake, and the robed prelate brandishing the cross before his eyes with the cry *Abjure! Abjure!* O'Casey recalls the books that his father used to 'read, pore and ponder over':

> . . . a regiment of theological controversial books, officered by d'Aubigné's History of the Reformation, Milner's End of Controversy, Chillingworth's Protestantism, holding forth that the Bible, and the Bible alone, is the religion of Protestants, with an engraving of the fat face of the old cod stuck in the front of it; Foxe's Book of Martyrs, full of fire and blood and brimstone, Popery Practical Paganism, Was St Peter Ever in Rome? having on it a picture of divines battering each other with books. . . .[24]

Many of these survive—more perhaps in attics than in bookshelves—in old houses around the country. Their combined effect was to nurture a picture of the Roman Church as an institution foreign, oppressive and menacing.

To this institution, as Protestants saw it, the Irish Catholic was absolutely subject. The doctrine of papal infallibility, proclaimed in 1870, made a deep impression on them. They conceived (as indeed did many ignorant Catholics) of this claim to infallibility as covering the whole range of human affairs; and they conceived of it as spreading downwards through the whole organism of the church, so that in the end no lay Catholic could controvert any priest on any matter whatsoever.

In this frame of mind it was not too difficult for Protestants to live on decent neighbourly terms with Catholics—as clearly most of them did—while retaining a wholesome dread of what these same Catholic neighbours might do if they were mobilised to action by their priests. As Russell wrote, 'In Ireland, no matter what the patriots say, men are Catholics first and Irishmen after. The Church is supreme when the real tug-of-war comes.'

Disestablishment, it was hoped, would take down the temper of religious controversy in an atmosphere in which, to use W. H. Gregory's phrase, 'only theological salamanders could exist'. It did indeed remove a grievance, but for members of the Church of Ireland it removed a psychological bulwark too. Their fears were sharpened, as we have seen, by the increasing involvement of the clergy in direct political action. Horace Plunkett saw the process in Galway: 'Priests in the polling booths—priests outside—priests marching their parishioners to the polls like Salvation Army processions.'[25] In the Home Rule debate of 1912 much use was made of the results of local elections to prove that Protestants could never hope for fair play in an Ireland dominated by the Catholic Church. Of six hundred members elected to local councils of Leinster, Munster and Connacht, it was stated, only eighteen were Protestant. Even a Protestant who stood far above the level of ignorant bigotry could feel that the domination of the church was baneful, not for Protestants alone, but for the independence of all Irishmen. T. W. Rolleston, a man with a deep sense of cultural nationalism, thought that the Nationalist Party had become the 'tame cat' of the church and saw 'more sincerity, more high-mindedness, more principle, and very much more education and interest' in the rising young men and women of Sinn Féin:

> They embody the rising force of resistance to clerical dictation in Ireland. The Bishops have reduced the Parliamentarians to mere puppets, but they have no influence at all over the Sinn Féin people, to whom a Bishop, when he is dealing with secular affairs, is no more sacrosanct than a magistrate. . . . Ireland needs a free and well-informed public opinion. It cannot have that as long as the Church holds its present position of authority over men's minds, and is able to ruin any Catholic professional man or trader who opposes it.*[26]

In fact Sinn Féin represented a strand in Irish political think-

* A marginal comment has been scribbled in pencil in the library copy of the book at the Royal Dublin Society: *See the anti-Catholic little bugger at work.*

ing which had existed ever since Wolfe Tone: a spirit of republicanism which was independent of the clergy, if not actively anticlerical, and was firmly opposed to sectarianism. It was represented in the Fenians; it survived in some fashion in the instinctive attitudes of Republicans as against Free Staters, Fianna Fáil as against Fine Gael. But it was always associated not only with republicanism but with radical political thinking. Protestants were clinging desperately to the status quo: even if they could have foreseen the victory of Sinn Féin, it would have been impossible for them to throw themselves into the arms of the Jacobins.

* * *

Underlying all Protestant attitudes—the very tap-root of prejudice—was a belief that religion was the mould of character. Catholics were dirty, lazy, thriftless, unreliable and ignorant. They were taught that it was no sin to tell lies to a Protestant or to steal from a Protestant. They were kept in ignorance so that their priests could hold sway over them. Protestants, according to this thesis, were on top because they were better, and they were better because they were Protestants. This sense of tribal superiority was always more marked among the Ulstermen; it was the basis of their demand for partition; it governed the politics of their statelet for fifty years, and led directly to the explosion of violence that marked its half-century. Even Roger Casement, who was to give his life for the Irish Republic, could write to another Northern Protestant: 'The Irish Catholic, man for man, is a poor crawling coward as a rule. Afraid for his miserable soul, and fearing the Priest like the Devil.'[27]

The whole attitude is crystallised in two words in the Home Rule debate of 1912. A member, pointing to the example of Co. Cavan, urged the Protestants of Ireland that 'they may repose perfect confidence in the patriotism and good feeling of their Catholic fellow-countrymen', and went on to assure the House:

If you went to a fair in Ireland you could not tell a Protestant from a Catholic.

From the benches opposite came the voice of the member for North Armagh:

I could.[28]

* * *

Mr W. B. Yeats did not take part in the celebrations of Her Majesty's Diamond Jubilee. On the same afternoon he attended a rival gathering called to organise the commemoration of the 1798 rebellion. His associates would not have shared the simple belief of the *Irish Times* that the spirit of the jubilee was in no way political, since it was 'not a declaration of any policy beyond that of Imperial unity'.[29] The group who set out to inflame the spirit of nationalism by the '98 commemoration were dedicated to fracturing imperial unity. Their concept of nationality was exclusive: a man who was loyal to Ireland could have no other loyalty. And thus they ruled out of participation in the nation those Irishmen who had grown up with a complex sense of nationality: loyalty to Ireland, loyalty to the Crown, and loyalty to the Empire.

To the majority of Protestants these loyalties were by no means incompatible with one another. They had been brought up to reconcile the contradictions. They felt no difficulty in cheering when Ireland beat England at rugby, and at the same time singing 'Land of Hope and Glory'. When they came to the lines

> Wider still and wider
> Shall thy bounds be set:
> God who made thee mighty
> Make thee mightier yet!

they saw themselves as sharing in the achievement of Empire. In its crude form this sentiment inspired the leader-writers of the *Irish Times* and the *Daily Express*, whose political comments must have been inexpressibly galling to anybody with a spark of nationalist feeling. And yet in its essence it was not ignoble. By background, by education, by family connections, Irish Protestants felt themselves part of an organism greater and more significant than their own little island. They believed in the mission of the Empire as 'a great world power making for peace, progress and civilisation'. Within that context they believed that Ireland itself could fulfil a larger destiny.

Such a philosophy was, of course, impossible to reconcile with the philosophy of Sinn Féin, which thought in terms of separate races, separate civilisations, separate languages. Rolleston saw the clash and believed that it must delay Home Rule.

The two Irish nations must first be made one before another frontal attack can have any chance of success. . . . Each of the nations of Ireland has laid hold of one side of a great truth, but neither has yet grasped the whole. One of them clings to the conception of Ireland's place and power in the Empire—the other to the conception of her separate individuality and freedom. Both are right and both are wrong.[30]

That was in 1900, when it still seemed possible that the two nations might be made one.

* * *

If there were two nations, there were some people who fell between them. 'A spiritually hyphenated people' is somebody's phrase for the Anglo-Irish; and by now one must begin to use this term, vague and exasperating as it is, if only for the sake of defining the indefinable. In general the Anglo-Irish were people born in Ireland who were of English origins, and were conscious of such origins: the consciousness is important. In general, too, they belonged to the upper classes: landlords were Anglo-Irish, but nobody ever applied the term to the lodge-keeper. To the Irish, the Anglo-Irish were marked out by a certain fashion of speech, a certain *hauteur* which was recognised as the manner of the 'quality'; and these characteristics were indelible, even if the individual were a clergyman's widow living on a pittance. If they stayed in Ireland they were not quite at one with the people. If they went abroad they said they were Irish, and usually said it with pride. A contemporary, discussing his own dilemma, writes: 'I myself feel Irish in England but often quite foreign in Ireland; no doubt having gone to school in England, another Anglo-Irish vice, has helped to strengthen that feeling of alienation.'

Schooling has something to do with it: it establishes loyalties early in life. Class has something to do with it. Blood has something to do with it, but not everything. Religion has something to do with it, but it is by no means co-terminous with Protestant. In the last resort, perhaps, you are Anglo-Irish if you feel Anglo-Irish, and that must mean feeling that you have a bond with two nations but belong totally to neither.

The Anglo-Irish Protestants prosecuted their search for identity in various ways. Standish O'Grady and Douglas Hyde—

both sons of the rectory—opened the door to a myth and a literature that the Irish could call their own. Yeats and his associates strove to create Irishness in English. Constance Gore-Booth, the 'new Irish beauty' who was presented at Queen Victoria's court in 1889, became the Countess Markievicz who marched out with the Citizen Army in 1916. When the Treaty debate came, she was one of the bitterest opponents of any concession to those of her own background and her own class: 'I, being an honourable woman, would sooner die than give a declaration of loyalty to King George and the British Empire.' Anybody who wanted to be treated as Irish must swallow the Republic, and swallow it whole.

But there were honourable men who thought that one might love Ireland without hating England; that one might make a commitment to the nation without rejecting the Empire. Of them all, Horace Plunkett is perhaps the most admirable. He was born into the full tradition of the Anglo-Irish aristocracy, and he grew up among people to whom fox-hunting was the serious business of life. Yet he devoted himself, almost with the single-mindedness of religious vocation, to the ideal of improving the life of the Irish people through agricultural co-operation. He put self-government second to self-respect, and he saw self-respect as the result of economic development. Plunkett was elected to parliament as a Unionist, but thrown out again by his Unionist constituents because he was not bigoted enough. Although he worked all his life for the Irish people, he never seemed to stand close to them: he found the Galway constituency 'illiterate, corrupt, and in every way disgusting', and he held that, although Home Rule was 'theoretically right, the people . . . *are not fit* for it'. His substantial achievements were the result of sheer driving conviction unaided by charm, eloquence or popularity. He did all he could to convert the Ulster Unionists from a policy of partition. He did all he could, as chairman of the Irish Convention of 1917, to bring about a settlement that would embrace the silent Ulstermen and the absent Sinn Féiners. 'He was', says his biographer, 'that intractable thing, an unyielding moderate.'[31]

Plunkett's epitaph inevitably carries overtones of irony. In Conor Cruise O'Brien's words, 'He lived to see his creameries burned by the English and his house burned by the Irish.'[32]

But his life is a testimony to the error of equating achievement with success. Edward MacLysaght, a wholehearted nationalist, has tried to explain how he saw the demands of nationality :

> If he was a Unionist at all he was one of that rare type which, while recognising the indisputable nationality of Ireland, has so little fear of its absorption or disappearance that the alleged material advantages of Union with England appear more desirable than the chances of self-government.[33]

*   *   *

In July 1914 Plunkett published a pamphlet in which he reminded the Ulster Unionists how 'in the Home Rule struggles of 1886 and 1893, they stood forth as the champions of the scattered minorities of their co-religionists in the South and West'.

> I shall refuse to believe [he wrote] that the Ulster Unionists are prepared to desert a quarter of a million of their fellow-countrymen, whose cause they formerly believed to be as sacred as their own.[34]

It was too late. It was too late to dent the saintly selfishness of the Ulstermen. It was too late to put up a fight for the scattered minorities. Within a week or two the Great War had begun. By the time it was over the world had changed and the Southern Unionists were no more than a scribble in the margin of history.

6

Rank on Rank to War

INSIDE the door of St Paul's parish church, just off the north quays of Dublin, there is a Roll of Honour of the parishioners and past members of the No. 8 Company, Boys' Brigade, who served in the Great War of 1914–18. The list runs to 269 names. Several families appear to have sent more than one son : there are three Ashtons, three Robinsons, three Radfords. One Ashton, one Robinson and one Radford are among the forty-seven marked with a red cross. These are the ones who died.

In August 1914 Irish loyalties were complicated. Fifteen years before, the mass of the people had been fervently pro-Boer; British defeats were cheered in the streets of Dublin, and services of thanksgiving for victory were held in Protestant churches only. But the Irish, as Shaw reminded them, had no reason to feel any sentimental attachment to Habsburgs and Hohenzollerns. The previous decade had been comparatively peaceful and prosperous. The struggles for the land had been ended, or almost ended, by Wyndham's Act of 1903, which effectively replaced the landlords by a system of peasant proprietorship. The Third Home Rule Bill, introduced in 1912 and delayed by the House of Lords, was nearing the end of the parliamentary steeplechase. The formula which it embodied was so restricted that it was hard to present it as the dream of 'a nation once again'. Nevertheless, there was a feeling that a principle had been gained : that movement for the future would be forwards, towards a more complete realisation of nationhood. That, at any rate, was the understanding of John Redmond, who had led the parliamentary fight for Home Rule; and on that understanding he was to stake—and finally to lose—his party and his career.

The Unionists on the other hand had taken their stand on the exclusion of Ulster (however that term might be defined) from the scope of Home Rule. Half a million Ulster Protestants had signed a Solemn League and Covenant to resist Home Rule, and they had demonstrated their resolution by forming a volunteer army and arming it with smuggled rifles. Regular officers stationed at the Curragh had intimated that they would resign their commissions rather than march against the North. The government began to look for compromise. The answer seemed to lie in exclusion—partial or total, permanent or temporary— of the area in which the Protestants could claim a majority. There was never the slightest doubt that religion was the dividing line.

Separatists too rejected the Home Rule Bill. They found its limited form of autonomy inadequate and insulting. As a counterpoise to the Ulster Volunteers the Irish Volunteers were formed to strengthen the hand of the South against the intransigence of the North. In the first months of 1914, as the sabres continued to rattle in Belfast, the roll of the Irish Volunteers rose from 10,000 to somewhere around 180,000. Guns were placed in these eager hands when a consignment of German rifles was run into Howth, near Dublin, by Erskine Childers and a group of conspirators who were largely—like him—Anglo-Irish, upper-class and Protestant.

Confusion, as Conor Cruise O'Brien has said, is the condition in which history exists. At this time it could profit only the extremist, who has the faculty of giving simple answers to complex questions. Southern Protestants in particular were at a loss to know where to turn. Their philosophy had been built on loyalty to the Crown and the Protestant religion. Now they found that loyal Ulster Protestants were prepared to resist the will of parliament by force of arms; that loyal officers holding His Majesty's commission would refuse to carry out unpalatable orders; and that His Majesty's Loyal Opposition was willing to countenance treason provided it was conducted on conservative principles. As for their religion, they found its ordained leaders calling down the blessing of God on the Covenant. The Bishop of Down and Connor declared that the Northern loyalists were not just fighting their own battle; they were 'the champions of that great multitude of Irish people in the South and West, both Protestant and Catholic, who dread Home Rule, knowing well what its nature would be, but dare not take adequate steps to

defend themselves'. The Rev. William McKean, a former
Moderator of the Presbyterian General Assembly, saw the
situation in plainer terms: 'The Irish question is at the bottom
a war against Protestantism. It is an attempt to establish a
Roman Catholic ascendancy in Ireland.'[1] Clearly the Almighty
would want to avoid any such perversion of the natural order.

Some of the diehards were ready to back Ulster to the hilt,
if only as a means of sabotaging the bill. 'We know', said Walter
Guinness, MP, 'that without Ulster—we can be quite frank—
Home Rule sooner or later must break down.'[2] The *Irish Times*,
which in general represented the professional and business classes,
found the idea of partition detestable; Unionists would endure
it 'as the only apparent means of saving our land and our
homes from the horrors of civil war'. The one point on which
all were agreed was that they could repose no kind of confidence
in the government, whether at Dublin Castle or at Whitehall.
'If we did not believe that the British Government in Ireland is
only sick and not dead,' said the *Irish Times*, 'we should be willing to concede that any other sort of government must be better,
or at any rate could not be worse.'

* * *

From this crisis of uncertainty the loyal Protestants were
rescued by the war. The European crisis had been moving across
the main news pages, but it was not until 29 July that it dis-
placed the Irish crisis as the lead story. On 3 August Germany
declared war on Russia. The next day the United Kingdom was
at war with Germany.

On the afternoon of 5 August, in a tense and emotional
House of Commons, John Redmond made the speech that began
the end of his career. The government, he said, might safely
withdraw all Crown forces from Ireland: 'Ireland will be
defended by her armed sons from invasion, and for that purpose
the armed Catholics of the South will be only too glad to join
arms with the armed Ulstermen.'[3] A few weeks later he went
further: he called on the young men of the Volunteers to
enlist for the war in Europe. He told the House:

For the first time—certainly for over one hundred years—
Ireland in this war feels that her interests are precisely the
same as yours. She feels, she will feel, that the British demo-

cracy has kept faith with her. She knows that this is a just war! . . . I would feel myself personally dishonoured if I did not say to my fellow-countrymen that it is their duty, and should be their honour, to take their place in the firing line.[4]

To the Southern Protestant Redmond's call brought a sudden vision of unity. It seemed to show, all at once, that the heart of Ireland was sound; that underlying all political issues there was the brotherhood of the Empire. To be sure, there were some dissidents. Sinn Féin denounced Redmond for betraying the national cause, and the Volunteers split. A few thousand, among them the hard core of the secret Irish Republican Brotherhood, rejected Redmond and formed a breakaway group. But the vast majority of the Volunteers, like the vast majority of the Irish people, seemed to be caught up in a sudden wave of enthusiasm for the war effort. On 5 August a crowd estimated at ten to twenty thousand turned up at the North Wall to cheer the reservists leaving for the front.

Ireland seemed really whole-hearted in the cause of Britain in those early days of conflict. Thousands rallied to the colours and people followed the fortunes of the war with the greatest interest. Theatres put on patriotic spectacles and not content with playing the British National Anthem, played 'Rule Britannia' as well![5]

The common threat and the common effort seemed to have bridged party divisions. At a Volunteers' meeting in Roscommon the parish priest, as chairman, read letters from two members of the local gentry offering to join the force. 'He thought they had reason to thank God that they had lived to see the day when influential Unionists like Captain Goff and Lord Crofton were willing to throw their weight and influence in with the Volunteer movement.' It should not be assumed, said the *Irish Times*, that a sudden solution had been found to Ireland's problems; but 'this new Irish unity, so strangely and so hardly achieved, will have results full of hope and blessing for Ireland'.[6]

* * *

Proudly you gathered, rank on rank to war,
As you had heard God's message from afar;

All you had hoped for, all you had, you gave
To save mankind—yourselves you scorned to save.

One of the deep dividing lines in Irish thought is the line
between those who remember the Great War and those who do
not. To the North, 1916 is the year of the Somme, the year in
which the Ulster Division was cut to pieces in a single summer
day. In every little town of the Protestant counties a war
memorial keeps the promise of remembrance. To the South,
1916 is the year of the Easter Rising, the year in which a
handful of men challenged the might of the British Empire,
and the Empire took in payment the lives of sixteen of their
leaders. There were a couple of thousand men, at most, involved
in the Rising. At the same time there were probably 150,000
Irishmen serving in the British forces. During the four years
of the war some half a million of the Irish joined up to fight,
and not less than 50,000 of them died.

Many were deterred, no doubt, by the bitter anti-recruiting
campaign waged by the republican press; and even loyalists
were infuriated by the chilly caution of the War Office, which
refused to grant the Irish units any badge or emblem of
nationality—it would stand for an Ulster Division but not for
an Irish Brigade. Lord Dunraven wrote afterwards that 'Irishmen would have volunteered to a man if it had not been for the
buckets of cold water that were thrown on them.'[7] In mid-
December, after four months of war, the response of Ulster was
much greater than that of the other provinces. Of the men of
military age in 1914, Ulster had sent 29·5 per cent. Leinster
came next with 15·7 per cent; Munster had sent 10·4 per cent,
and Connacht only 4·4 per cent. All the same, by the autumn
of 1915 over 80,000 men had volunteered, and to these must be
added some 52,000 Irishmen in the regular army and the reserve.

The story of the Irish regiments in battle is stirring to anyone
who has a regard for human courage; the record of their losses is
heartbreaking. A battalion of the Munsters was wiped out before
it was a month old; Dublin, Munsters and Connaught Rangers
were cut to pieces in the mad adventure of Gallipoli; the 16th
Division was overwhelmed in the German advance of 1918,
losing 7,000 men in two weeks. Month after month the casualty
lists streamed through the columns of the newspapers.

All this, or most of it, has been obliterated from the folk-memory of the South. History was made, in the end, by the handful of Volunteers who turned their backs on Redmond. Their insurrection, hopeless and heroic, placed a new group of leaders in charge of Ireland's destiny. What history they did not make has been forgotten, except by the scattered remnants of Protestants who still turn out to sing the memorial hymn on Armistice Day:

> O valiant hearts, who to your glory came
> Through dust of conflict and through battle flame;
> Tranquil you lie, your knightly virtue proved,
> Your memory hallowed in the land you loved.

* * *

The war presented the Southern Protestant, never a very sophisticated political animal, with a simple ideal and a simple duty. The Anglo-Irish were by tradition officers and gentlemen. When the call came they voluntered at once, and the casualties were appalling. Douglas Hyde wrote in 1915 from Roscommon:

> Nearly everyone I knew in the army has been killed. Poor young Lord de Freyne and his brother were shot the same day and buried in one grave. The MacDermot of Coolavin, my nearest neighbour, has had his eldest son shot dead in the Dardanelles. All the gentry have suffered. *Noblesse oblige.* They have behaved magnificently.[8]

But sacrifice was not confined to the gentry. The small men, the clerks and shop assistants, the members of No. 8 Company of the Boys' Brigade, enlisted along with the landlords' sons and paid the same toll. Everything in their background had prepared them for this duty: the portraits of the royal family in the parlour, the stories in *Chums*, the echoes of Kipling and 'Onward Christian Soldiers', the National Anthem itself, bracketing God's enemies with the King's.

Sacrifice, of course, was not confined to Protestants. But the Protestant community, true to its own traditions, seems to have contributed much more than its proportionate share. By late 1915 there were about 80,000 Irish Catholics in the forces and 53,000 Irish Protestants. In 1917, out of a total enlistment from Ireland of 150,000, some 90,000 were Catholic and 60,000

Protestant.[9] From 25 per cent of the population the Protestants had supplied 40 per cent of the men. If the proportions remained the same for the duration of the war, then Protestant Ireland must have put about 200,000 volunteers into the field over four years. And if the Southern Protestants enlisted at the same rate as those in the North, then some 30,000 Southern Protestants must have gone to the war. For a community which numbered no more than 175,000 men, this was a remarkable effort. It goes far to explain the debility of the community in the years after the war, when so many Protestant homes were peopled only by women.

The men who were over age for the fighting forces threw themselves into the recruiting campaign, while their womenfolk prepared 'comforts for the troops'. This concentration on the war diverted their attention from politics—which they had always preferred to leave to the government anyway. It has been suggested that their co-operation with Nationalists on recruiting platforms may have encouraged some Unionists to revise their estimate of the Irish situation: they may have begun to think co-operation possible in a wider context. Unionist organisations in the south and west faded away because the active men went to the war, and there began to be talk of 'bowing to the inevitable'.[10]

* * *

But what exactly was the inevitable? Protestants thought of it in terms of the Home Rule Bill at most; and indeed, true-blue Unionists were determined that even this was unacceptable. Many would have agreed with John Gregg, the Bishop of Ossory, that the experience of war showed that 'Ireland's geographical position determines inevitably that it can never be a sovereign state'.[11] What was more important was that the bill had been rejected out of hand by the Sinn Féin wing of the national movement. That section of the Volunteers which had broken away from Redmond contained the most ardent and vigorous spirits in the movement. While 30,000 of their comrades put on British khaki and set off for the front, they remained at home to prepare the real battle against the real enemy. They had on their side an able group of propagandists who could not be quenched by an ineffectual censorship. They had against them an inept government which dissipated Irish goodwill by its grudging attitude towards the Irish troops and by its constant mutterings about conscription. In the end the spark was set to this resistance by the 1916 Rising and the executions that followed.

The Rising, when it came, aroused deep anger and resentment among the loyalists. They felt it as a stab in the back at a time when the fearful losses of nearly two years of war had caused all who considered themselves British to feel that they were fighting for their lives. In January Gallipoli had been abandoned after almost a year of fruitless fighting and terrible losses. In France the armies were locked together in the trenches, the troops growing stale and bitter as they waited for the reinforcements that would launch the big push and tip the scale at last. In this situation of desperate balance the Rising appeared as a treacherous attempt to aid the enemy. With the benefit of aftersight, it is easy to forget the importance in contemporary eyes of the link between Germany and the rebels—the link represented by Roger Casement. Alison Phillips, the loyalists' historian, wrote in 1923 :

> The rebellion was certainly no mere desperate adventure of a few hot-headed youths, which was from the first foredoomed to failure. It had been carefully planned with the aid of the best military brains in Europe, and but for a series of accidents—fortunate or unfortunate, according to the point of view—it might well have succeeded in effecting all that the Germans expected of it, namely, the enforced withdrawal of a very large body of British troops from the Western front at a very critical period of the war.[12]

Most loyalists, no doubt, were in favour of executing the leaders : the *Irish Times* expressed their view—and was never forgiven—when it called for the surgeon's knife. They did not, perhaps, have in mind a surgeon who would keep sawing away for ten days; but they would have thought Shaw blasphemous when he wrote : 'All the slain men and women of the Sinn Féin Volunteers fought and died for their country as sincerely as any soldier in Flanders has fought and died for his.'[13] Treason was treason, rebellion was rebellion; and punishment was punishment. 'This is no time for amnesties and pardons; it is a time for punishment, swift and stern,' wrote Archbishop Bernard of

Dublin to *The Times*. 'And no one who lives in Ireland believes that the present Irish Government has the courage to punish anybody.'

Nationalists seemed as shocked as loyalists, at first, by the 'reckless and barren waste of life, courage, property, and the historic beauty of a capital city'. The *Freeman's Journal* found some cause for congratulation in the part played by the Irish regiments against the insurgents: 'The 4th and 10th Dublins kept the glorious anniversary of their regiments' heroic landing at Sedd-el-Barr by defending their own city against the blind, self-devoted victims of the hun.'[14] In the House of Commons John Redmond expressed his 'detestation and horror', and claimed to speak for the overwhelming majority of the people of Ireland. So he did; but not for long. Within a few days the executions began to turn the tide of public opinion. And as people saw the flutter the Rising had caused in the dovecotes of Downing Street, they began to see it in a new light. 'Within a few weeks', says Alison Phillips, 'popular sentiment in Ireland had completely swung round, and the rebellion was converted, from the Sinn Féin point of view, from a disgraceful failure into a glorious success.'[15]

* * *

The new balance of power was defined in the general election which followed the armistice in December 1918. Of 105 Irish seats 73 were won by Sinn Féin, 26 by the Unionists. The Nationalist Party was all but annihilated. Apart from the two Dublin University seats, no Unionist was elected outside Ulster.

The Sinn Féin members boycotted the Westminster parliament to which they had been elected. Instead they formed an assembly in Dublin and declared it to be the sovereign parliament of Ireland. It was a brilliant manoeuvre in all respects but one. The Unionist members naturally ignored the summons to attend; and by their absence they seceded, in effect, from an independent Ireland. Thus, though the First Dáil claimed jurisdiction over the whole of Ireland, its very existence defined partition.

In the years that followed loyalists could look back with nostalgia on the short period when Irish unity seemed to have been attained. The mood is well caught in a report in the *Irish Times* of November 1921 on the unveiling of a memorial at Thiépval to the men of the Ulster Division:

> In those great and terrible days there was no 'partition' between the soldiers of the six counties and those of the twenty-six. Ulstermen, Leinstermen, and Munstermen fought and died together. Almost within the shadow of the Ulster Memorial lies a little cemetery where 'the Connaughts' sleep. Many good Irishmen, among them John Redmond and his brave brother,* hoped and prayed that the common sacrifice, the common heroism would heal the discord of centuries, and that the *via dolorosa* of Messines and Thiépval would lead us to the gateway of a United Ireland.[16]

---

* John Redmond's brother, William Redmond, MP, joined the Royal Irish Regiment at the age of fifty-four and was killed in action in 1917.

7
The Cold Grey Light of Dawn

T H E new Ireland of 1922 was not the Ireland of anybody's dreams. For Sinn Féin, heirs to the dream of 1916, it was a compromise: instead of an all-Ireland Republic, they had twenty-six counties and dominion status. The loyalists were still able to claim a nominal allegiance to the Crown and the Empire; but they had lost the fight for the Union, and they had been cut off from the Protestant North. The Orangemen had come nearest to getting what they wanted, and in doing so had set everybody else an example in intransigence. They had six counties, not four (Tyrone and Fermanagh, always marginal, had been thrown in as a makeweight), they had got rid of any time-limit on partition, and they had a promise from London of no coercion.

There had never been very much love lost between the Protestants of the North and those of the South. Belfast was the boom-town of Victorian Ireland, a rapidly growing centre of manufacturing industry with a population that outstripped Dublin. Its civic leaders had the aggressive self-confidence of the magnate whose wealth is as the wealth of ten because his heart is pure. Dublin by comparison had become a junction between London and the Irish hinterland. It was a centre of administration and professional life, a centre of commerce and exchange, but only in a very elementary way an industrial city. Dublin had the airs and graces, but Belfast held the purse. There was common ground between the landed gentry—all pressed into the same creases by the public schools and the army—but in the North they had to identify themselves with the prejudices of the middle-class and working-class Protestants, in order to hold Unionism together in simple opposition to Home Rule/ Rome Rule. In England and Scotland the urban working classes were starting to vote Labour. The trick-of-the-loop in Northern politics was to keep them voting Conservative.

From a fairly early stage the Southern loyalists were aware that the Ulstermen would have few scruples about tossing them overboard if the ship appeared to be making heavy weather. Nevertheless, as they came face to face with the demand for independence, they had to accept that their only hope of commanding respect by weight of numbers lay in unity with the Protestants of the North. Logically their policy must be one of conciliation : they must attempt to reach an accommodation that would satisfy nationalist demands without precipitating partition.

At the Irish Convention of 1917–18 Lord Midleton and his small group of Southern Unionists tried to work towards such an accommodation. The more pragmatic Protestants—those who felt, for better or worse, that their roots were in Ireland—understood that the Union was no longer in question. The question for them was whether they could assure security for their families, respect for their property and genuine freedom for their religion in the Ireland of Sinn Féin.

From 1918 onwards they were negotiating for their future with the 'men of no property'. The new rulers of Ireland, it was evident, were not going to come from Eton and the Guards : they were emerging, uncreased, from the small farms and the national schools. Most of them, probably, would have dismissed Midleton and his allies as contemptuously as Ernest Blythe—himself a Protestant from Armagh : 'We looked on them as the dregs of landlordism.'[1] Nevertheless the Sinn Féin movement had never been sectarian in its thinking. It was opposed to Protestant Ascendancy, but not to Protestants. In the years that followed this boundary of principle was blurred, for many of the rank and file, by jealousies and antagonisms. But the men who were now reaching out to grasp control of their country's government had enough statesmanship to recognise that the minority had a contribution to make to the Irish nation. They believed, too, that by fair treatment of the Southern Protestants they would win over the stubborn loyalists of the North.

If the British cabinet had been able to recognise the Dáil which assembled in Dublin in January 1919 as a constituent assembly, representative of the majority of Irishmen, the misery of the next four years might have been averted. Very likely, if such a settlement had been mooted, the Southern loyalists would have thrown their weight against it: they were not yet ready for 'surrender'. But when Lloyd George finally brought forth the Treaty and was challenged to say what had made such a settlement acceptable in 1921 when it was unacceptable in 1918, the only truthful answer was: war.

* * *

The Sinn Féin policy was to treat the vote in the general election as a plebiscite in favour of national independence. But at the first session of Dáil Éireann, summoned in Dublin in January 1919, that plebiscite was translated into terms which were to create a deep and lasting fission in the new state. The twenty-seven members present* adopted a declaration which ratified 'the establishment of the Irish Republic'. The Republic they had in mind embraced thirty-two counties and was totally separated from Britain. That it was unrealisable was, for the moment, beside the point. What mattered at this time was how the situation presented itself to the rank and file of the Volunteers; and this view is given in its awesome simplicity by Tom Barry:

> The Rising of 1916 was a challenge in arms by a minority. This was a challenge by a lawfully established government elected by a great majority of the people. The national and the alien governments could not function side by side, and one had to be destroyed. All history has proved that, in her dealings with Ireland, England had never allowed morality to govern her conduct. Force would be used to destroy the Government of the Republic and to coerce the people into the old submission. There could be no doubt it would succeed unless the Irish people threw up a fighting force to counter it.[2]

So Barry—who had served his apprenticeship to war in the British Army—set out to make war on his old masters. This was no romantic gesture like the Rising of 1916. The country boys

---

* Of the 105 constituencies, 32 returned Unionists or Nationalists, who declined to attend. Of the 69 Sinn Féin members (representing 73 constituencies), 34 were in prison, and eight others were unable to attend. For a bitter but perceptive account of the proceedings, see P. S. O'Hegarty, *A History of Ireland under the Union, 1801–1922*, London 1952, 725 ff.

were tough, ruthless and realistic. The campaign which they unleashed began with the murder of a few policemen and developed into a full-scale guerrilla war. Its object was to break down the rule of British law throughout Ireland. In May 1920 the *Irish Times* acknowledged its success: 'The King's Government has virtually ceased to exist south of the Boyne and west of the Shannon.'

They were grim and terrible days for the whole country, but especially perhaps for Protestants in the rural areas, who now saw about them the collapse of their entire social order. Their loyalty remained, as it had always remained, with the Crown and the Empire. Their instinct was to support the King's government, even when they thought that government weak and ineffectual. They had always been on the side of the law because the law had always been on their side. Now they found that their law—British law—was set aside; a rebel régime had turned the concept of order upside down, so that loyalty became treason and treason loyalty. For a generation which identified war with Flanders and Gallipoli it was impossible to accept the new definitions: to see labourers in cloth caps, in ambush behind a ditch, as a national army; to recognise a local policeman—generally an Irishman and a Catholic—as 'the enemy'; to understand that a loyalist who followed his instinct to give help to the Crown forces was a 'spy'.

At the Somme Haig had lost 20,000 men in a single day. The casualties of two and a half years of war in Ireland are reckoned to be under 2,000. But this is the perspective of the academic historian; it bears no relation to the feelings of those who lived through month after month of death and destruction. Indeed, the small, almost personal scale of the events often gave them a special sense of outrage. Lionel Fleming's father, who was rector at Timoleague, recorded in his diary 'a long list . . . of those whose big houses were destroyed in a night—the fire-raising squad being sometimes led by a servant or gardener who had worked with them for years'.[3] Horror was aroused in particular by some of the individual killings: of Alan Bell, an elderly magistrate who was dragged from the Kingstown tram and shot before the eyes of the other passengers; of Sir Arthur Vicars, a retired civil servant, besieged and shot dead in his home in Kerry; of Dean Finlay, a clergyman eighty years of age, done to death on his own front lawn. It was hard—it is still hard—to dignify deeds like these as 'acts of war'.

As it became evident that no protection could be expected from the authorities, loyalists began to move away from the danger areas. Lady Gregory noted

> an exodus from the County [Galway]. The Goughs leave this week and Lough Cutra is to be shut up until they see how things are, and Hugh is still in the Irish Guards. Lord Killanin has had trouble at Spiddal and has dismissed all his men and gone to London. The Lobsdells, because of their motors having been searched or put out of action the night they were going to the Roxboro dance, are going to live in England. Amy has let Castle Taylor and lives in England.[4]

It was the breakup of the old county society. Many of the houses left unoccupied were burned out and never rebuilt.

Faced with an elusive enemy, the military had no answer except a policy of reprisals. This was intensified from mid-1920 with the arrival of the Black and Tans and the Auxiliaries, the emergency forces enlisted by Lloyd George from among the ex-soldiers of the Great War, and now let loose upon Ireland. Their mission, in principle, was to restore law and order. In practice, they were sent to stamp out insurrection by terror, and their callous brutality has earned them a special place of hatred in the Irish folk-memory. Moreover, the policy ignored the fact that many of the loyalists were themselves virtually hostages to the IRA. The troops avenged themselves for an ambush by burning out a few houses and then moving away. The IRA promptly met reprisal with counter-reprisal: they selected the country house of some prominent loyalist and sent it up in flames.

Protestants tended to think that they were specially singled out for these attentions. Tom Barry, who led the famous West Cork flying column, writes that 'The majority of West Cork Protestants lived at peace throughout the whole struggle and were not interfered with by the IRA.'[5] But the price of peace was silence. They had to keep ears, eyes and mouth closed; they had to keep their opinions to themselves. More terrifying than the ambushes of troops or attacks on police barracks were the 'executions'. John Good, a well-to-do farmer from the Bandon area, was shot dead on his own doorstep by masked raiders. A few weeks later his son's body was found in a ditch, a bullet through the head; and eventually the widow and daughter, too, got notice to quit, and had to flee to England leaving all their belongings behind them. Good may have been, in IRA terms, a 'spy', giving information to Crown forces; but locally there remained a nasty suspicion that he was the victim of a land war, picked out by envious neighbours as part of a deliberate campaign to drive Protestants off the land. A similar suspicion was felt at Dunmanway, where seven leading Protestants were shot within two days. At Coachford a seventy-year-old widow, Mrs Lindsay, was condemned to death for giving information on an ambush. The two viewpoints are concisely illustrated by the index references in two standard works. Dorothy Macardle (*The Irish Republic*) lists 'Lindsay, Mrs, Coachford, Co. Cork, executed 1921'. Alison Phillips (*The Revolution in Ireland*) lists 'Lindsay, Mrs, murdered'.

Tom Barry held that it was British policy to put a sectarian twist on all such information. If the individual killed by the IRA happened to be a Protestant, his religion was always stated; if he was a Catholic, no mention was made of religion. This policy was 'in keeping with the general British propaganda to make Protestants of Ireland believe that they and their faith would be victimised and destroyed under a Republican Government of Ireland'. Barry himself was above suspicion of religious bigotry—like many republicans, he kept a place of honour in his pantheon for Tone and the Ulster leaders of '98. But the Protestants themselves, understandably, read the situation in simpler terms.

In its essence the war was one which it was impossible to win. The IRA was sustained by dedication, by comradeship, and by the almost total support of the people. On the other hand, they were amateur soldiers, and after a couple of years the strain began to tell on men and resources. On the British side, it might in theory have been possible to field an overwhelming force which would grind down any conceivable resistance; but liberal opinion in Britain, and world opinion in general, were already strongly against the British government.

As for the Southern Unionists, or those who were left, they

D

had lost any remaining confidence in Dublin Castle and Whitehall. Bryan Cooper—one of the few who went on, after independence, to take an active part in the political life of the new
state—expressed the disgust of many:

> In the last year they have seen the power of the law over-
> thrown, the police rendered powerless, the troops concentrated
> in the larger towns, and their lives and property left at the
> mercy of anyone who cared to assail them. . . . Side by side
> with the realisation that the Government is either unable or
> unwilling to protect them is coming the yet more startling
> discovery that on the whole Sinn Féin is trying to prevent
> anarchy and maintain order. . . . Thieves have been appre-
> hended, welshers punished, persons endeavouring to use
> intimidation for their own private means dealt with as 'bring-
> ing discredit on the Irish Republic', and this has made a con-
> siderable impression on the Unionist mind.[6]

What the minority wanted, more than anything, was law and
order. And if it was clear that it could not be British law, then
they were prepared to accept the law of an Irish parliament.
By 1921, moreover, they had no further hope of solidarity with
the greater block of Protestants in the North. The Government
of Ireland Act (1920), a dead letter in the South, had become
operative in the North: partition was now a *fait accompli*. Once
Britain decided to cut her losses, the future of the Protestant
minority would be in the hands of the Catholic majority.

In June 1921 that step was taken. Lloyd George wrote to de
Valera to suggest a conference. The *volte-face* was startling to
those loyalists who still believed that the government would
never submit to 'the disgrace of making advances to men whose
hands were stained with the blood of servants of the Crown'. It
advertised, to those who still had any illusions, that in the last
resort London would never jeopardise British interests for the
sake of a handful of sentimental colonists. De Valera's response
was, in the circumstances, statesmanlike and reassuring. He at
once invited five leaders of Irish Unionism to discuss the form of
his reply to Lloyd George: 'The reply which I, as spokesman
for the Irish Nation, shall make to Mr Lloyd George will affect
the lives and fortunes of the political minority in this island, no
less than those of the majority.'[7] It was significant, for those

with a taste for reading portents, that he defined the minority as political, not religious. Four of the five Unionists accepted the invitation, thus accepting, implicitly at least, de Valera's claim to speak on behalf of 'the Irish Nation'. From the four-day conference there emerged the truce of July 1921 which paved the way for the Treaty in December.

* * *

'One of the most deplorable desertions of their supporters of which any Ministry has ever been guilty': this, in retrospect, was Lord Midleton's bitter verdict on the Treaty.[8] Yet it is difficult to see what more could have been won for the minority. For their property they were to have the same protection as any other citizen. For their religion they had a guarantee of 'freedom of conscience and the free practice and profession of religion, subject to public order and morality'. Instead of the obsolete Union, they had the status of a dominion within the Commonwealth, with a Governor-General in Dublin to represent the King. The negotiators from the Dáil had gone as far as they could, and much further than they wished. It was soon to be evident that for many of those who had sworn the oath to the Republic they had gone too far.

Midleton had wanted 'safeguards'—in particular a Senate with a guaranteed representation of Unionists, enjoying powers not much unlike those of the old House of Lords. Alison Phillips was more realistic :

> With the establishment of the Free State the *raison d'être* of Unionism in Ireland had come to an end, and it is difficult to see how Unionists, as such, could be represented. The true lines of cleavage are religious, social, and, to a certain extent, racial, and it is not thinkable that, under modern conditions, any one of these divisions could have been given separate representation.[9]

There were others—less legalistic or more trustful—who saw that the only worthwhile safeguard for the minority was goodwill. On the day after the signing of the Treaty Arthur Griffith, as Minister for Foreign Affairs, published a letter in which he gave a firm assurance for the new government :

> We desire to secure the willing co-operation of the Unionists, in common with all other sections of the Irish nation, in

raising the structure and shaping the destiny of the Irish Free State. We look for their assistance in the same spirit of understanding and goodwill which we ourselves will show towards their traditions and interests.[10]

The gesture was accepted in the spirit in which it was made. A few weeks later, after the Treaty had been ratified—narrowly enough—by the Dáil, the *Irish Times* stated its position; and it must have spoken for a great many of those loyalists who still looked to a future in Ireland :

> Mr Griffith promises that it [the Provisional Government] will recognise no distinction between Irishmen, that it will provide every guarantee for 'fair play all round', and that it will strive to make an end of the old causes of jealousy and hatred. The Irish people will not expect the impossible, but they will welcome any honest and patriotic substitute for the recent régime of drift and disorder. We desire for Southern Unionists no better guarantee than the guarantee of 'fair play all round'. The goodwill of the majority will be a more potent safeguard of their interests than any written promises. The security furnished by just laws, firmly enforced, is the only security that they demand, and it will be useless to them unless they share it with all their fellow-countrymen. As a political organisation, Southern Unionism has ceased to exist. As a large body of educated, patriotic and mainly conservative Irishmen, the Southern loyalists hope to do their part in shaping their country's future. The Provisional Government will not appeal to them in vain.[11]

* * *

Peace, however, was not yet in sight. Within days Mr de Valera had repudiated his envoys and the Treaty which they had signed. Before the spring of 1922 was out the Volunteers had split. The anti-Treaty section set out to destroy the Dáil which had ratified the Treaty, and the Provisional Government which it had set up. In June 1922, when the constitution of the Free State was published—'a magnificent charter of liberty', in the view of the *Irish Times*—the new state was already torn by civil war. By the time the anti-Treaty forces laid down their arms, in May 1923, the country had been scarred from end to end by death and destruction; Arthur Griffith and Michael

Collins were both dead; and the new state had come to birth amid a bitterness more intense, because more intimate, than all the bitterness of the past.

In this perilous situation all the fears of Protestants were revived. In May 1922 the Archbishop of Dublin led a deputation from the General Synod of the Church of Ireland to wait upon Michael Collins, to inquire of him 'if they were to be permitted to live in Ireland, or if it was desired that they should leave the country'.[12] The Provisional Government was reassuring, but it could not answer for the IRA Irregulars; and as the campaign continued there seemed no doubt that it was directed especially against the persons and property of Protestants. Former Unionists who had accepted seats in the new Senate (the Earl of Mayo, the Earl of Granard, the Countess of Desart, Sir Bryan Mahon, even Sir Horace Plunkett) had their mansions burned out, with a desolating loss of fine furniture and works of art. Between January 1922 and the spring of 1923 some 140 burnings of country houses were reported. But, though the landed gentry suffered most conspicuously, there were plenty of humbler victims. Thus at Ballinasloe in mid-1922 there were reports of an organised campaign to drive Protestants out of the district:

> On Monday Mr Salter, manager in Mr Woods' boot establishment, received notice to leave the town. He has since left. Mr Swan, a Protestant who lives in Clonmore with his wife and family, and is agent for Messrs Guinness, received a final notice to leave. Mrs J. Rosin, a Protestant widow residing at Clonmore with her 18-year-old daughter, a linesman named Davidson, and Mr W. Crawford, the station-master, all of whom are Protestants, have been warned.[13]

Reports of the same date tell of intimidation of Protestant farmers in Leitrim and Monaghan. Lady Gregory saw the exodus from Galway: 'Furniture vans engaged for nine months ahead are taking goods from the country to England.' The new state was still unequipped to give protection to its citizens, and loyalists complained bitterly that they had been disarmed and left without any means of defending themselves by a British government which then withdrew and abandoned them without a backward glance. It must be said that efforts were made, both by clergy and politicians, to check intimidation. The outrages against Protestants in Ballinasloe were vigorously condemned by the parish priest as 'uncharitable, un-Christian and un-Irish'. Frank Fahy (later a member of Mr de Valera's party in the Dáil) said on an election platform that he did not want the votes of men who persecuted others on account of their religion : 'The seizure of grass lands and the persecution of Protestants was done by selfish people for selfish ends.' Liam Mellows, an out-and-out republican who was later to be executed by the Free State, said : 'It did not matter whether a man was a Protestant or a Catholic, so long as he believed in the freedom of Ireland.' This was, once again, the voice of Tone.

But for very many Protestants, high and low, it now appeared that the invitation to make a contribution to building the new state was a mockery and that they must seek their future elsewhere. The columns of advertisements of estates for sale tell their own story. In the *Irish Times* of 16 June 1922 a butler (Protestant, married) announces that he seeks a situation, and adds : 'England Preferred'. No doubt he saw little scope for his talents in the new Ireland.

8

'Part and Parcel'

These people are part and parcel of the country, and we being
the majority and strength of the country . . . it comes well
from us to make a generous adjustment to show that these
people are regarded, not as alien enemies, not as planters,
but that we regard them as part and parcel of the nation,
and that we wish them to take their share of its responsibilities.[1]   KEVIN O'HIGGINS (1922)

O v e r fifty years have passed since Kevin O'Higgins, in these
words, sketched the policy of the new government towards the
Protestant minority: fifty years of independence, under the
name of Free State or Republic. In that time their numbers have
run down by something between forty and fifty per cent, so that
they now make up a good deal less than the traditional five per
cent of the community. Although their stake in the country,
in terms of property and employment, is still substantial, their
voice is rarely heard. Their approach to public life is tentative
and wary. It is time therefore to ask whether the fine words of
Kevin O'Higgins really mean what they said. Has the Irish
state given the religious minority a fair opportunity to participate on an equal footing in the life of the nation? Is the minority
at fault for failing to embrace the opportunity offered?

In approaching these questions we shall find ourselves caught
up in a dichotomy which dates back at least as far as O'Connell
—the dichotomy between the state and the nation. The state is
an institution constructed on liberal democratic principles, committed to cherishing all the children of the nation equally. The
nation is a mass of people bound together by some sense of
spiritual identity; and the great majority of these people have

been moulded by the Roman Catholic faith and by an ethos which is rural and (however distantly) Gaelic. Nations which have enjoyed a long period of statehood have had the opportunity, so to speak, to grow institutions suited to their own climates. In Ireland, where institutions to a great extent have been borrowed from another society, the problem of the state has been to strike a balance between instinctive beliefs and rational convictions.

It is no harm to begin by stating the obvious, because it is only against the background of the obvious that one can begin to make fine distinctions. Protestants were accepted as equal citizens in the new state; and the law reflected the will and demeanour of the people. There were individual cases of outrage or discrimination, but these are remarkable mainly as exceptions to a general pattern of conduct. Protestants kept their jobs, their homes, their property, their savings. They kept their own institutions—their schools, their hospitals and the like— and these institutions received perfect parity of treatment from the state and its servants. The Protestant churches and their property were handled with kid gloves; it is amusing, in retrospect, to look back on the dire warnings of oppression and expropriation that were sounded throughout the Home Rule debates. Fifty years after independence the Church of Ireland still has two cathedrals in Dublin, and the Roman Catholic Church has none. It is not easy to think of another case in which a defeated ascendancy has been treated with such exemplary generosity by a victorious people. An Irish democracy converted a privileged minority into an equal minority, not into an underprivileged or subservient minority. Most of its problems—real and imagined—arose from the fact that the minority itself was too tiny and too scattered to exercise any influence through the normal machinery of democratic government.

O'Higgins had called upon the Protestant minority to 'take its share of the responsibilities' of running the country; and it is not unfair, perhaps, to say that it still had a somewhat exalted view of what its share ought to be. The habits of a ruling class die hard. William T. Cosgrave, the first President of the Executive Council, did his best to meet its expectations. He had the power to nominate thirty members—one-half of the chamber— to the first Senate. Of his thirty names, more than half were

Protestant. Taking nominated and elected members together, there were twenty-four non-Roman Catholics on the roll of sixty. With a few exceptions—such as J. G. Douglas, a Quaker businessman, who had been a trusted friend of Michael Collins, and W. B. Yeats, the nation's most distinguished man of letters —they all came from the Unionist camp. Lord Glenavy (formerly James Campbell), who had been a Unionist MP for fifteen years, was elected Chairman. Among the most active members were Douglas (who was elected Vice-Chairman) and Andrew Jameson, the distiller, who had been an associate of Lord Midleton's in the Irish Convention, and had worked consistently for a decent settlement. The confidence which these men inspired by their personal qualities is illustrated by the fact that, when Mr de Valera wanted to negotiate a cease-fire in the civil war, he invited Douglas and Jameson to act as his intermediaries with the government. Lord Midleton himself had refused a nomination; but the Senate included seven peers, two baronets and a knight. If the President's choice tended to overrepresent the gentry, it is hard to blame him: these were the people on whom the Protestants themselves had depended as their spokesmen.

The Senate gave the Protestants a voice, but it had little or no real power. In the Dáil, where the power lay, they had to win their seats by the normal process of democratic election. Proportional representation, which had been seen as one of the safeguards for a minority, might have made a difference in Northern constituencies; but in the South, in general, the Protestant population was so scattered that it could not register as a voting force. In the event nine Protestants were elected on a roll of 153. One of them was a former Unionist MP, Bryan Cooper, elected for South County Dublin—one of the few areas where the Protestant vote was significant. Dublin University elected two members who tended to be regarded, *ex officio*, as spokesmen for the minority.* In the absence of the Ulstermen there was never any prospect of a Protestant *bloc* in the Dáil, and in fact there was never any attempt to form a front or faction representing the minority. In the constituencies some effort was

---

* It is of some interest, as an index of changed times, to note that, of the three senators elected for Dublin University in the present Senate, two are Catholics.

made to mobilise Protestant votes for Protestant candidates, but the Protestant Association in Monaghan was the only formal organisation with this objective. On the whole, the leaders of Protestant opinion felt that no step should be taken which would tend to polarise political life on sectarian lines.

Within a few years both the administration and the parliamentary organs of the state had given a lesson to those who said that the Irish were unfit for self-government. The Cosgrave administration may be criticised on many grounds, from timidity to ruthlessness; but it managed to lift the machine of the state out of the ditch and put it back on the road with the new driver at the wheel. In the new situation the support of the Protestants went overwhelmingly to President Cosgrave. The substance of government policy was to restore law and order, to build an administration and to reconstruct an economy crippled by years of war. Its financial principles were as orthodox as those of the Bank of Ireland, and it had no very revolutionary social ideas. With such a programme, essentially pragmatic, the members of a mainly conservative minority were unlikely to quarrel. They set at that time a pattern of political attitudes which has remained constant almost down to the present day: a pattern of voting for the status quo lest worse befall. If this policy seems excessively timid, it should be remembered that a minority is rarely in a position to be adventurous. It seeks security, not change.

* * *

While it would be wrong to underestimate the magnanimity of the government's policy, it was not, of course, formed without calculation. In the first place it was deemed important to win back as quickly as possible the confidence of investors; and nobody was unaware that Protestants still occupied a dominant position in the world of commerce and finance. It was well worth while, therefore, to secure the trust of men like Jameson, whose judgment would influence not only Irish but British business interests in regard to their investment in Ireland. There was, besides, the consideration of the North. At the time when O'Higgins spoke, nobody—certainly nobody in the South—supposed that there would still be a border in Ireland in another fifty years. By behaving generously to the Protestants of the South, it was thought, the government would win the confidence of the Northern Protestants, and bring a speedy end to partition. Some members of the Southern minority were themselves anxious to work towards this solution. In 1925 J. G. Douglas joined a group of Protestant senators—mainly ex-Unionists—on a mission to Belfast, with the object of interesting Northern businessmen in a form of federal unity.[2] But so far as the Northern Protestants were concerned, they had now secured a sealed-off majority, and partition was for ever. The resulting deadlock over the border issue and the breakdown of the Boundary Commission of 1925 ended any hopes of a major adjustment. Only by an act of faith, hereafter, could Protestants in the South see themselves, or be seen by their fellow-citizens, as representatives of a twenty-five per cent minority of the Irish nation. They spoke—if they uttered at all—with the voice of five per cent.

The minority, moreover, had been desperately weakened by the war and its aftermath. The census of 1926 showed that the Protestant population had fallen by one-third in fifteen years; and the crude figure by no means represents the nature of the loss. The war had taken almost a whole generation of young men. After the war there had come the exodus from the country and the country towns. Those who went were not only the old and frightened: often they were the remnant of those who were young and confident enough to think of making a new life in another country. The people left behind were 'the old, the cautious, and the conservative. . . . There was little clear leadership, and the general policy adopted was "Lie low and say nothing." '[3]

John Gregg, who had become Archbishop of Dublin in 1920, represents in himself the dilemma of many Protestants confronted with the fact of the new state. By origins, by education, by conviction he was an establishment man to the core. When the Treaty separated Ireland from Britain he felt (in his daughter's words) 'as if he had been banished from the Garden of Eden'.[4] Yet he had to make an attempt to assert some moral leadership of a community whose political leadership had evaporated. A week before the Treaty he had stated the claim of Southern Protestants to take some part in the negotiations (he was ignored by Lloyd George, who took a godly view of small battalions). Gregg argued:

As a minority we differ from the majority in ethos, and although we are as truly Irish as many in the other camp, the differences are so marked as to cause us to seem alien in sympathy from the more extreme of our fellow-countrymen. . . . Singularity is never popular. It arouses a certain jealousy, and very small occasions are sufficient to provoke antagonism. . . . Whatever our religious or political outlook may be, here is our home, and we have every right to be here.[5]

What Gregg had foreseen was that, while the official policies of the state might be beyond reproach, they might not be altogether consistent with the sentiment of the nation. By the 1920s Ireland was already weaving her national myth, using three main threads—the republican, the Catholic and the Gaelic. To each of these the Protestant ethos was alien. As the myth gained in strength it became more and more difficult to believe in a Protestant identity which was also Irish.

For people who, under the old régime, had been impeccably orthodox, it came as a shock to find orthodoxy changed. They had no training in resistance. Instead they tended to step back from public life and expend their energy in exclusively Protestant charitable works, where they could feel a sense of community. The public face indeed expressed a dignified acceptance of the new order. Bishops urged their flocks to be good citizens of the Free State; the Fellows of Trinity College declared their allegiance. But private opinion still hankered for the old days. Anglo-Ireland, Lennox Robinson wrote, 'brought to bear on the young Government every prejudice that snobbery and religion could evoke. . . . It sneered at their wives, at their clothes and at their manners.'[6] Lionel Fleming said of the mass of his co-religionists:

They did not regard the Irish nation as having anything to do with them. It had to be accepted, of course, as the system to which one must pay one's income tax, but they would never, until the end of their lives, speak of its government as 'our government'. In spite of the supposed treachery of Britain, their flag remained the Union Jack, and their anthem 'God Save the King'.[7]

In the context of myth, symbols like these mattered more than substance. The new state, busily weaving its own myth, had chosen for its national anthem a brassy ballad which extolled the victory over the ancient enemy:

> Soldiers are we, whose lives are pledged to Ireland;
>   Some have come from a land beyond the wave.
> Sworn to be free, no more our ancient sireland
>   Shall shelter the despot or the slave. . . .

A minority still predominantly loyalist could hardly be expected to share these sentiments. Their characteristic rite was the annual celebration of Armistice Day, when the service of commemoration for the dead became a grand rededication to King and Empire. Ironically, the poppies which were sold in aid of disabled ex-servicemen were themselves the focus of a petty war. Poppies were worn not only to aid the cause or to commemorate the fallen, but as a gesture of defiance. Trinity lads set a razor-blade in the lapel behind the poppy, so that anyone who tried to snatch it would slash his fingers.

* * *

The clash of symbols was capable of producing violence throughout the decade. Shops or offices which displayed the Union Jack—even among the flags of the League of Nations— were liable to be invaded by bands of young men who felt it their national duty to tear down the imperial emblem; and in 1928 a harmless insurance official named Armstrong, who had given evidence against such a group, was murdered by gunmen. Intimidation of juries and witnesses made it almost impossible to enforce the law. Protestants in general accepted that the government was trying in good faith to give them the protection to which they were entitled; but they would have been exceptionally stupid or exceptionally brave if they had failed to take the hint. People who did not embrace republican orthodoxy found it healthier to keep their mouths shut.

The pressure of Catholic orthodoxy was exercised, as we shall see in a later chapter, to mould the law itself in a manner which would make it conform with the official Catholic conscience. The champions of the Gaelic orthodoxy had to be content with certain ritual steps taken to establish the place of the Irish language in the national life. The state called itself *Saorstát Éireann*; it declared Irish its official language, it printed its documents bilingually, and it put a word or two of Irish on the new stamps. Most Protestants found this procedure faintly ridiculous : men who would have been ashamed to boggle over *zeitgeist* or *wagon-lit* made strangulated noises when confronted with *Dún Laoghaire*. When the Senate debated whether its opening prayer should be said in English or in Irish, Yeats, who had drawn so much of his early inspiration from O'Grady's versions of the Irish sagas, protested at 'the histrionics which have crept into the language movement. . . . People pretend to know a thing which they do not know, and which they have not the smallest intention of ever learning.'[8] The Senate was not unique : only a few words of Irish were used in either House, and not many of the members would have understood it anyway. As for the Protestants, they were firmly wedded to their English-language heritage. Few had the imagination to see that the gestures, ineffectual as they might be, did represent a kind of hunger in people who felt that they had been robbed of their birthright and who were anxious to make up that loss to their children.

In 1926 the Cosgrave government introduced Irish as a compulsory subject in national schools, and made a pass in Irish a requirement for success in the higher school examinations and for entry to the public service. Since most Protestants thought of education in practical terms as a passport to a good job, they saw in this policy a form of disguised discrimination. There was indeed no very good reason why the Irish language should be easier for a Catholic than for a Protestant. But there was a feeling that it 'belonged' to Catholics; it was taught with missionary zeal by the Christian Brothers, while in Protestant schools, in general, it was taught badly and was resented equally by pupils, teachers and parents. Certainly it acted as a barrier—psychological or actual—against the entry of Protestant youths into the public service, and in this way it contributed to their sense of alienation and to the continuing emigration of young Protestants in search of jobs.

In the substance of domestic administration there was little cause for complaint. The guarantees of religious liberty embodied in the constitution were amply fulfilled. But domestic administration was one thing and long-term constitutional objectives were another. At the time, the anti-Treaty side zealously promoted the idea that the Free Staters were lackeys of the Empire and had sold out the Republic. This is not at all the picture that emerges from a study of the Treaty debates and the events that followed. While the government took pains to behave correctly under the Treaty, its view of that document differed fundamentally from the view held by the remnant of the loyalists. For the loyalists the Treaty was a terminus. For the new rulers it was merely a stage on a journey. It was not the best agreement that could be imagined, but it was the best that could be secured. The freedom which it conferred was, in Collins's words, 'not the ultimate freedom that all nations aspire and develop to, but the freedom to achieve it'.[9]

The new leaders—even those who pressed the case for the Treaty most forcefully—therefore looked forward to using it as a lever to loosen the link with the Crown and the Empire. For the loyalists, on the other hand, its major compensation was the forging of a new and, it was hoped, more durable link. Nobody, said the *Irish Times*, would welcome the Treaty more gladly than the Southern loyalists:

> For them Ireland does not exist, and never will exist, apart from the Empire which the blood of their sires and sons has cemented. If Ireland accepts the Empire with her heart, and not merely in the cautious wording of an oath; if she accepts them as Imperial Irishmen, they will come joyfully to her side. The Southern loyalists' gifts of education, character and experience are essential to the building up of a new nationhood. They will rejoice to put these gifts into the common stock.[10]

Between those who accepted the Crown conditionally, and those who would not accept it at all, the choice of loyalists was clear. But conditional acceptance fell a long way short of loyalty. This difference of understanding underlay all the civilities that marked the opening of the new era.

* * *

In the first ten years of self-government, under President Cosgrave, the Protestant minority developed a considerable degree of confidence in the goodwill and good faith of the Free State government. This was, however, tempered by a general caution, for they were by no means certain how far the government represented the attitude of the people, and there was always a certain fear that the wind might change. In this sense they remained a foreign body embedded in the tissue of the nation—a foreign body which might at any time set up local inflammation.

Prejudice, in short, was not dead. A practical demonstration was given in 1931 in the celebrated case of the Mayo librarian.

The Local Appointments Board (a body set up to remove all suspicion of jobbery from local appointments) advertised the post of librarian for Co. Mayo. The advertisement stated, as was customary, that a competent knowledge of Irish was required for the post. Following the usual competition the board appointed Miss Letitia Dunbar-Harrison, who was a Protestant and a graduate of Trinity College. The local library committee refused, however, to accept Miss Dunbar-Harrison, giving as its reason the fact that she did not have the required knowledge of Irish. The county council passed a resolution to the same effect. The Minister for Local Government (General Mulcahy) ordered an inquiry. When he established to his satisfaction that the council was improperly refusing to implement the appointment, he accordingly dissolved it and appointed a commissioner to exercise its powers.

The debate which ensued in the Dáil forms a connoisseur's guide to prejudice in Ireland. It is characteristic of it that books were spoken of throughout as if they were dangerous drugs; and the central issue really had nothing to do with Miss Dunbar-Harrison's competence in Irish, but turned quite simply on one question—could a Protestant be trusted to hand out books to Catholics? It is worth noting, moreover, that this question was canvassed most actively by the members of Fianna Fáil (Mr de Valera's party), who had entered the Dáil four years earlier under the republican banner and declared their faith by making an annual pilgrimage to Wolfe Tone's grave at Bodenstown. Thus Mr P. J. Ruttledge (later Minister for Justice) argued that

> It has to be recognised that in the Co. Mayo, where practically 99 per cent of the people are of a certain religious persuasion, a person in the position of librarian must feel, as any person who holds definite religious views must, that these views must be portrayed in some way in the distribution of

books. What may appear to a member of one religion as being perfectly all right may appear to a member of another religion as being completely wrong.[11]

Mr Richard Walsh wanted to disavow any suggestion that his party was anti-Protestant :

> We are not a party of bigots. But neither I nor any member of the Fianna Fáil party in the Co. Mayo or in this Dáil apologise to anybody for being Catholics or for taking up a Catholic attitude on a question of vital importance to Catholic interests. If the Minister thinks he is going to cow the people and the priests of Mayo in this matter he is making a great mistake.

Mr Michael Clery sought for 'the hidden hand' behind the minister and found it in 'the *Irish Times* and the Masons and Unionists, the people with the purse behind the Minister'.

Mr de Valera himself (who was to become President of the Executive Council in the following year) did nothing to discountenance these attitudes :

> I say that if I had a vote on a local body, and there were two qualified people who had to deal with a Catholic community, and if one was a Catholic and the other a Protestant, I would unhesitatingly vote for the Catholic.

Other things, of course, being equal. If the work, Mr de Valera went on, was to be considered as 'active work of a propagandist educational character', then the people of a county where over 98 per cent of the population was Catholic were justified in insisting upon a Catholic librarian.

'The Deputy', said the minister, 'has gone as near saying as constitutionally he can that no Protestant librarian should be appointed to county libraries in this country.' The minister had the votes to carry the day, but it was a hollow victory. Miss Dunbar-Harrison was appointed but met with organised local hostility, and it was not long before she was transferred to a less sensitive post.

What is most remarkable, perhaps, at a range of over forty years, is that the government of the day was prepared to face such pressures, political and clerical, in order to assert the equal rights of the minority. Nevertheless, as the shadow of Mr de Valera loomed larger, Protestants found themselves increasingly hemmed in by the three orthodoxies—the republican orthodoxy, the Gaelic orthodoxy, and now the Catholic orthodoxy. It is all the more remarkable that, within twenty years, they found themselves in the position of supporting Mr de Valera, because he was seen as the only man strong enough to take a stand against the bishops.

9

From Free State to Republic

T HE process of constitutional enlargement undertaken by the
Cosgrave government did not cause much affront to the sentiment of the sometime loyalists of the South, since it was nego-
tiated within the context of the Commonwealth and it maintained the symbolic link with the Crown. They shared in the
national pride at the recognition of the Free State by the League
of Nations, and they admired the part played by Irish statesmen
in the evolution of the Statute of Westminster, the foundation of
the new-style Commonwealth. Indeed, it is not too much to say
that they began to acknowledge the new leaders as statesmen
only when they were recognised in that role by the Commonwealth and the outside world.

They saw a threat to this progress towards respectability in
the advent of Eamon de Valera. The leader of the anti-Treaty
faction had led his party into the Dáil in 1927 (with a swagger,
as the newsreels show, very unlike the grave demeanour of his
later years). To do so he had been obliged to devise a formula
which would enable him to satisfy himself that he was not
taking an oath, and to break with the republican purists who
would tolerate no compromise. He was, however, still supported
by the IRA, at this stage a strange association of socialist
revolutionaries and anti-British zealots, held together by their
common hatred of the Cosgrave administration and their common readiness to use the gun. It was understood that if de
Valera came to power he would use his position to advance the
sacred cause of the Republic; and by 1932 it was evident that
this was no remote possiblity. The *Irish Times* spared no effort
to bring out the Protestant vote against him:

There is the duty of self preservation. If Fianna Fáil takes

office, the wealth and security of every citizen, including the
ex-Unionists, will be impaired and, perhaps, gravely imperilled. There is a duty of loyalty to Ireland and to the
Empire. If Fianna Fáil takes office, the Free State's carefully
fostered prosperity will wither, and she will become an
Ishmael from that Empire which the ex-Unionists, their sons
and their ancestors have helped to mould.[1]

In ten years the minority had learned to live in the Irish state—
securely enough, if not without many a backward glance to the
Good Old Days. De Valera threatened them with a régime
which would be more republican, more Gaelic, even more
Catholic. They feared not only a tampering with the delicate
constitutional fabric, but cultural isolationism, economic isolationism, and the elevation of violence once again to the status
of law.

The tide had turned, however, and in 1932 Mr de Valera
became head of the government—an office which he continued
to hold, apart from two three-year spells of coalition government, until his election to the presidency of the Republic in
1959. It was not very long before the Protestants began to
discern that de Valera in office was a very different animal from
the one that had seemed so dangerous in opposition. The
'economic war' with Britain caused some casualties among businessmen and farmers, but in a personal sense Protestants found
themselves just as secure in person and property under de Valera
as they had been under Cosgrave. Two years after the accession
of Fianna Fáil Dr Gregg, the Archbishop of Dublin, said at the
opening of a teacher-training college that 'he could not have
expected more in the way of courtesy and goodwill than he had
received from the government of the Irish Free State';[2] and in
1936 the *Church of Ireland Gazette* judged that the party 'has
had the rough edges knocked off it, and has sobered down almost
unbelievably'.[3] A little heat, which some found alarming, could
be provoked on symbolic occasions: when George VI was
crowned, Dublin cinemas were prevented from showing the
coronation film by threats of violence. (The film went on circuit
instead around the Protestant parish halls, and made a vast
amount of money for church funds.) But the government's problems with its own extremists were recognised: 'A great deal of

the government's professed hostility towards Britain has been eyewash,' the *Gazette* said. 'The extreme element in Fianna Fáil had to be placated at all costs.'[4]

* * *

Mr de Valera, however, was pursuing his own course with his own relentless logic. The Free State existed by virtue of an act of a British parliament. An old republican could accept the legal and moral status of an Irish state only when it was constituted by the Irish people. The new premier's first step was to abolish the oath of allegiance to the Crown and diminish the status of the Governor-General. But while he was thinking his way towards a formula for total dissolution of the link with the Crown, he was presented out of the blue with a splendid opportunity by the abdication of Edward VIII in 1936. The abdication left a constitutional vacuum. The Irish government took advantage of it to rush through legislation which, in effect, deleted the Crown from the constitution of the Free State for all domestic purposes, leaving it only as 'a symbol of co-operation' between members of the Commonwealth.

The speed and dexterity of this manoeuvre gravelled all opposition. In the Dáil, Deputy Thrift, who represented Dublin University, protested against the government's haste: 'We have here introduced, under the plea of urgency, revolutionary legislation—legislation which scatters to the wind all care or forethought for the wishes of the minority and gives them practically no opportunity of airing their views or putting forward their case.'[5] The *Irish Times* was almost maudlin: 'The link with the Crown is the most precious possession of those Irish citizens who combine an abiding love of their own country with an almost mystical attachment to the British throne.'[6] This feeble reaction was an index of the disarray into which the sometime loyalist ranks had fallen.

The 1930s in Ireland was a period of extreme confusion—for those who lived through it, as for those who try to study it at the range of a generation. The IRA, launching into the Fianna Fáil régime virtually as a licensed private army, became such a menace to the state that de Valera himself was obliged to take action against it. The constitutional party of ex-President Cosgrave (reorganised in 1933 as 'Fine Gael') went to pieces in opposition, and expended its energies on a futile fling with a kind of decaffeinated fascism. In this situation Protestants tended more and more to dissociate themselves from political life. It was still, broadly speaking, unthinkable to support Fianna Fáil; and if it was futile to be in opposition, to be a Protestant in opposition was doubly futile. Their most significant political comment was made with their feet. In the two decades 1926–46 their numbers fell by 25 per cent; their emigration rate was consistently higher than the rate for Catholics, and the emigrants included a large number of young people. Those who remained tended to armour themselves in a carapace of contempt for all things Irish. In the era of industrial protection they pined for British goods, and lamented the shoddiness of the Irish substitutes. My father, the most scrupulous of citizens, closed his eyes when my mother marched three children home through the customs, after a holiday 'across the water', in three pairs of new English shoes.

* * *

If there was, nevertheless, a Protestant presence in the public arena, this must be put down largely to the transformation of the *Irish Times*. By background and tradition, the paper was Protestant and Unionist: its enemies called it West British. Its standard leading article is summed up by in a nationalist novel of the 1900s as 'a homily on the inferiority of the Celt, with a thanksgiving that the Ascendancy are not as other people'.[7] On the other hand, it was not half bigoted enough for hardline Unionists. It was deeply committed to the concept of the 'Imperial Irishman'. It was opposed to the Catholic Church functioning as a political organisation; but it was ready to take a Presbyterian to task for the same reason:

We have always assumed that Churches historically connected with Ireland are resolved to continue their work there under any circumstances, and therefore ought not to identify themselves with any particular form of government. We feel that no Church is entitled to bind all its supporters to a political creed—much less to a political collect. In his sermon at the Ulster Hall on Saturday, Dr McKeon claimed for the Church a right to lay the Divine measuring-line on every attempted form of legislation bearing on the character, the freedom and the well-being of the people. We think that this is a very dangerous claim for Churches which denounce the doctrine of infallibility.[8]

These lines were written about the Ulster Covenant in 1912; but a perfectly clear continuity of thought appears in the paper's stance—forty years later—on the crisis over the Mother and Child health scheme.

As the people it represented dwindled away after 1922, the *Irish Times* itself might have been expected to wither and die. Instead it made use of its freedom from ties to church or party in order to carve out a new niche in a changed society. Of the two other national newspapers one was afflicted by a paralysis of piety, and the other was the official mouthpiece of Fianna Fáil. The *Irish Times*, with no visible means of support, was able to assume the role of *franc tireur*. For a generation after the Treaty the public was dependent on it for any full and consistent *exposé* of information and controversy on such matters as censorship and divorce.

This role was fully developed after 1934, when R. M. Smyllie took over the editorial chair. 'This was the man', says a writer who worked under him, 'who had done more, probably, than anybody to persuade the Irish Unionists, small in numbers, but disproportiontely influential owing to their wealth and their social standing, to come to terms with the Irish Free State.'[9] Smyllie, himself a man of fairly conventional attitudes, had a style and individualism that made him a magnet for the brighter talents of the period. His achievement, as editor, was that he made a Protestant newspaper a necessity for Catholics too. For some Catholics, that is; for the *Irish Times* was by now largely catering for a Dublin intelligentsia: the professional men, the young civil servants, the academics, the writers: the men and women of the university generation who were dissatisfied with orthodoxy. 'Slowly but surely', wrote a critic in 1945, 'it is becoming the organ of the entire professional class, Protestant and Catholic. . . . The class it speaks for may or may not be moribund, but the *Irish Times* is ten times more alive than its rivals in the newspaper world.'[10]

The vitality was sometimes whimsical and sometimes perverse, but at its best the paper performed a vital service for at

least a generation: it refused to let the concrete shell of orthodoxy set hard around Irish society. In this way it contributed
to the development of the very different society of the 1960s
and 1970s, in which the newspaper itself has been able to
enlarge its role and greatly increase its readership, though in
doing so it has, perhaps, ceased to speak with the distinctive
voice of a Protestant community.

* * *

The *Irish Times* and Mr de Valera were at one, oddly
enough, on one of the great issues of the 1930s. When the
Spanish Civil War broke out the *Irish Times* sent a correspondent to report from the government side; it was obliged to
withdraw him under pressure of cancellation of advertising by
all Catholic schools. The Catholic Church was prepared to
regard Franco's campaign as a holy war, and a section of the
Blueshirt movement—the idiot child of Fine Gael—set out for
Spain to fight against godless communism. De Valera, however,
insisted, against all clerical pressure, on a policy of non-interven-
tion. This first indication that he was willing to stand firm
against pressure from the Catholic Church was not lost on
Protestants. It may well have contributed to their placid acceptance of the special recognition accorded to that church in the
constitution of 1937.

The purpose of the constitution was, in Mr de Valera's terms,
to legitimise his own position; it was important less for the
provisions written into it than for the fact that it was enacted
by the people, by way of plebiscite, and thus disposed finally of
any suggestion that Ireland held her independence by licence
from Britain. Constitutionally, it created a republic in all but
name. It contained no reference to the Crown; it embodied a
claim to jurisdiction over the whole island of Ireland, and it
recognised ('the statement of an obvious fact', said the President)
the 'special position' of the Roman Catholic Church. The history
of this article, Article 44, will be discussed in the next chapter.
All that need be said here is that no objection was made to it
by the other churches; it did not in any way diminish their
rights or create a new established church.

Protestants in general did not appear to feel that the constitution imperilled their status, either political or religious. 'The
new Constitution is largely bunkum, and to that extent it is

harmless,' the *Irish Times* concluded;[11] and the *Church of Ireland Gazette* concurred: 'The whole thing will not make us any freer, will not indeed make the slightest difference to our affairs.'[12] The reality of contact with Britain was not affected. Irishmen still travelled back and forth across the Irish Sea without any form of passport control. They were still eligible for jobs in Britain, even in the civil service or the armed forces. They could still, in certain cases, hold British passports. If they lived in Britain, they were even entitled to vote and to stand for parliament. Not many people cared about the constitutional niceties of the 'dictionary republic' so long as this access to Britain was preserved.

Under the new constitution the presidency became a ceremonial office, 'above politics'. By an act of deliberate policy, the government secured agreement from all parties to the nomination of a Protestant, Dr Douglas Hyde, the veteran founder of the Gaelic League. A service to mark his inauguration was held in St Patrick's Cathedral. Mr de Valera, now Taoiseach (Prime Minister), did not attend. He might hold office under a Protestant head of state, but, as a loyal Catholic, he might not attend a service in a Protestant church.

* * *

In some strange way the war years saw a melting down of traditional prejudices in the Irish Protestants. They still supported the British cause, to a man, and many went to join the armed forces; their names appear often on the war memorials in country churches, as an epilogue, so to speak, to the great sacrifice of 1914–18. Wartime censorship caused some resentment, because its commitment to 'balance' in the public press led it to suppress any hint, however slight, of sympathy for the Allied cause. But there was fairly general acceptance that the government's decision to remain neutral was unavoidable. Sir John Maffey, British representative in Dublin in the war years, wrote:

> It is remarkable how even the 'pro-British' group, men who have fought for the Crown and are anxious to be called up again, men whose sons are at the front today, loyalists in the old sense of the word, generally agree in supporting the policy

of neutrality for Éire.* They see no possible alternative.[13]

For the first time, quite a number of Protestants expressed their commitment to their own country by volunteering for the Irish army or the part-time defence forces. At the same time—perhaps because they had to rationalise their decision not to go out and fight—those who stayed at home began a new self-examination, a search for an Irish identity. By now a younger generation, which had grown up since the Treaty, had emerged from school; and to these young Protestants the traditional loyalty was already second-hand. They did not feel that intense attachment to King and Empire which had been cherished by their elders. Some of the younger Trinity men—W. B. Stanford, D. A. Webb, H. R. McAdoo—published pamphlets which showed a new awareness of their role, as churchmen and citizens, in Irish society.

Up to the war Protestants had built up a tradition of voting for Fine Gael—the old Cosgrave party—because it was seen as more 'pro-British' than Fianna Fáil. Now, as motivations became more complicated, it would have been logical to see a dispersal of Protestant support around the points of the political compass. In fact, however, Fine Gael succeeded, in three years of coalition government, in driving almost the whole of Protestant sentiment to the opposite pole. The arrival of a new party, Clann na Poblachta, with a radical republican policy, acted as a catalyst in party politics. At the general election of 1948 Fianna Fáil was returned in a minority position, though still the largest party; a hasty coalition formed under the leadership of Mr John A. Costello of Fine Gael took over government. Soon after it came to power the coalition—determined to show itself more republican than the republicans—repealed the External Relations Act of 1936 (see page 105) and declared the state formally to be a Republic. The announcement was made by Mr Costello on a visit to Canada, where he informed the astonished Irish people, through a press conference, that Ireland was no longer a member of the Commonwealth. The British government, it emerged, had been given no advance informa-

---

* The state was officially designated Éire in the 1937 constitution. Although the title was soon abandoned, it was seized on joyfully by the Northern Unionists, who now had a political term distinct from the geographical one. From this point they spoke (and still speak) of Ireland as an island divided between Ulster and Éire.

tion, and Mr Attlee had to introduce legislation at once to avoid making foreigners of the Irish in Britain. As a makeweight —and perhaps out of sheer irritation—the Attlee government gave a positive guarantee that the status of Northern Ireland would not be changed without the consent of the Northern Ireland parliament.

The severance of this last formal bond with the Crown was carried out in a fashion so maladroit as to cause the greatest possible affront to everybody concerned. For the loyalist minority the whole business was unforgivable. Their faith in Fine Gael was finally undermined three years later, in what is now known as the Mother and Child crisis. Dr Noel Browne, the young Minister for Health in the coalition, proposed to bring in a free health service for mothers and children. The scheme was condemned by the Catholic bishops as contrary to church teaching. Costello dropped Browne like a hot brick; Browne published in the *Irish Times* the correspondence between them, and the government fell. In the ensuing election de Valera came back to power. Within a couple of years his government quietly introduced a health scheme not very unlike the one which the coalition had so ignominiously abandoned.[14]

For Protestants the message was clear. Fine Gael had cringed at the flourish of a crozier. De Valera had 'stood up to the bishops'. What the minority wanted was a civil power which would set a boundary to the expanding power of the Catholic Church. De Valera was their man. If the contest was to be between republican principle and Catholic principle, then the sometime loyalists were going to end up on the republican side.

'The Catholic Nation'

Reluctant as we are to criticise other religious groups, it seems necessary to point out that at present a concerted effort is being made by the religious minority to secure a dominating position in our public life. One has only to read a succession of pronouncements from their spokesmen to see that this is true. Offensive statements about the Church have now become common form with them. They claim that leadership in every community belongs to a minority, and, recalling their long ascendancy here in the past, they assert that they should be the dominant group here today. They recognise that they have positions of influence out of all proportion to their numbers, and in the same breath they exhort their members to secure more leadership and power. It is of course a leadership in thought and ideals that is in question, not mere personal prominence.

I suggest that this is an explicit challenge to a Catholic nation which it would be unwise to overlook. Even if it does not succeed in making us desert our faith it may do much towards neutralising our Catholicity, and preventing the application of its principles. It may have done much to this effect already. We are opposed by an extremely efficient propaganda machine. We may have reached a stage when calling Ireland a Catholic nation will itself be regarded as a challenge, and even deplored by some Catholics.[1]

Most Rev. WILLIAM PHILBIN, Bishop of Clonfert (1957)

O N E of the dominant themes of national thinking during the formative years of the state was the concept of Catholicity. It is better to borrow this rather vague term from Bishop Philbin's address quoted above than to speak of the influence of the

Roman Catholic Church, because we are speaking not so much of a structured intervention by church leaders in civil affairs as of a climate, an atmosphere, an ethos. The principle of equal rights for all citizens was guaranteed by the constitution and it was never called in question by the people. At the same time zealous Catholics felt it natural that the public policies of an independent Ireland should be pervaded by a Catholic philosophy. In the North they spoke of 'a Protestant parliament for a Protestant people'. In the South it was commonplace to speak of 'a Catholic nation'.

Even in 1957, as the bishop surmised, there were already a good many citizens, among the majority as well as in the minority, who questioned this description. It was, as they saw, rarely 'the statement of an obvious fact'. It was always, in one way or another, a declaration. It always seemed to carry some unspoken codicil, some implication that only Catholics belonged to the nation as of right, all others on sufferance. Dr Philbin himself was regarded, at this period, as one of the more progressive social thinkers in the Roman Catholic hierarchy. Some of his listeners may perhaps have wondered at his presentation of a handful of docile Prods as 'an extremely efficient propaganda machine'; but they could hardly have failed to get the message. The minority is being told to keep its place; and the place of a minority is a minor place.

In its official policies, as we have noted, the state took care not to discriminate between citizens. But among its leaders one can detect the note of schizophrenia; and this runs through Fianna Fáil as well as Fine Gael. A recent writer has suggested that, despite their claim to be the heirs of the republican tradition, 'Some of the published statements of Mr de Valera and his colleagues imply that, to them, the only true Irishmen were Catholics.'[2] The mental attitudes underlying such statements have been decoded by Dr Conor Cruise O'Brien:

The real answer lies in the peculiar nature of Irish nationalism, as it is actually felt, not as it is rhetorically expressed. The nation is felt to be the Gaelic nation, Catholic by religion. Protestants are welcome to join this nation. If they do, they may or may not retain their religious profession, but they become, as it were, Catholics by nationality. Recognising, as they must, at least the overwhelming primacy and preponderance of the Gaelic and Catholic component of the nation, they are not expected to quibble or jib at such a statement as 'We are a Catholic nation.'³

Given this frame of reference it was not inconsistent for statesmen, while representing the whole nation, to show the utmost deference towards the Roman Catholic Church and its leaders. Mr Cosgrave's government established the papal nuncio as permanent doyen of the diplomatic corps. Mr de Valera's first cabinet, on taking up office, sent a message of 'respectful homage and good wishes' to Pope Pius XI. Mr John A. Costello and his colleagues went still further in terms of filial piety :

> On the occasion of our assumption of office and of our first Cabinet meeting my colleagues and myself desire to repose at the feet of Your Holiness the assurance of our filial loyalty and of our devotion to your August Person, as well as the firm resolve to be guided in all our work by the teaching of Christ, and to strive for the attainment of a social order in Ireland based on Christian principles.⁴

It was inevitable, given this context, that the thinking of the church would be reflected to some extent in the policies of the state. On the whole the influence exercised by the church was rather less than either its champions or its enemies would have predicted. Home Rule did not turn out to be Rome Rule, and Protestant citizens did not feel their rights infringed. But Catholic thinking was reflected positively in certain measures which affected the personal rights of citizens : notably in the laws relating to censorship, divorce and contraception. Finally the state's recognition of the church was enshrined in Article 44 of the 1937 Constitution.

These laws were not in any sense directed 'against Protestants'. But the state did—to a limited extent—carry into the civil code the moral teaching of the Catholic Church; and by doing so it limited the freedom of conscience of all citizens. The censorship of publications, established in 1929, represents in the clearest possible fashion the enshrinement of a certain narrow moral code, then held to be Catholic, in the laws that governed Irish society. The chairman of the Censorship Board, for the greater part of its career, was a Catholic clergyman, but it was not—in law at any rate—a religious censorship: it was not in any way parallel to the Roman Index. It was empowered to ban any publication held to be 'in its general tendency indecent or obscene', as well as any book or journal that advocated 'the unnatural prevention of conception'. For almost thirty years it issued its lists of banned books month by month, relentlessly scorching the green shoots of all the world's literature. By 1954 it had protected the fair flower of Irish youth from contamination by nine Nobel prize-winners, and it had excluded works by almost every serious contemporary Irish writer. The practice of the board was reformed from 1956, when new members were appointed with a judge of the Circuit Court as chairman; and in 1967 Mr Brian Lenihan, as Minister for Justice, carried a new act which limited the ban on any book to twelve years. At one stroke he released a vast reservoir of dammed-up literature—around 5,000 books. In subsequent years the censorship has dwindled from a major scandal to a minor nuisance.[5]

* * *

In the debates surrounding these controversial topics, Protestants were generally ranged on the 'liberal' side. This does not mean that they tended either by reason or emotion to the left: as a group, they were for the most part conservative in their views on the social order. But between Catholics *en bloc* and Protestants *en bloc* there existed, all the same, a difference which it is tempting to define as the difference between *rurality* and *urbanity*. Rurality centres on an unchanging code of manners and morals; it takes its rulings from the past and projects them to the future; it argues that what was good enough for my father is good enough for me. This was (it is changing) very much the ethos of the Catholic Church in Ireland. By contrast, the ethos of the Protestant was that of the townsman who sees change as constant; to whom all decisions are provisional; who sees that *autres temps* mean *autres moeurs*. The underlying importance of Mr Lenihan's reform of censorship in 1967 was its acceptance of the principle that standards change.

I propose, in what follows, to pass over censorship, which is no longer an issue of serious controversy; to look severally at the laws relating to divorce and contraception; and to end with a note on Article 44 of the 1937 constitution. The reader should bear in mind that Article 44 has been amended,* and that the law on contraception is in a state of flux. A situation that was frozen solid for a generation at least is now beginning to melt; and as the thaw sets in the speed of the flow may be astonishing.

Divorce

There has never been any explicit provision for divorce in Irish law. The Matrimonial Causes Act of 1857, which admitted divorce *a vinculo* (i.e. with the right to remarry) was never extended to Ireland. When the Irish Free State came into being and took over the body of common law then in force, a person domiciled in Ireland had no way of seeking a dissolution of his marriage except by the antiquated and costly procedure of a private bill in parliament.

In 1925 Mr Cosgrave's government decided to bar this door. In doing so it was, of course, giving effect to the ruling of the Catholic Church that marriage is indissoluble by civil process. Its method was to pass through the Dáil—with the minimum of fuss—a resolution to the effect that private bills for divorce would no longer be entertained by the House. It then called on the Senate to carry the same resolution.

The scene was now set for a debate which has become celebrated for the speech of Senator W. B. Yeats. 'It is one of the glories of the church in which I was born', he said, 'that we have put our bishops in their places in discussions involving legislation. . . . The living, changing, advancing human mind sooner or later refuses to accept this leglislation from men who base their ideas on the interpretation of doubtful texts in the Gospels.' He went on to this resounding peroration :

> I think it tragic that within three years of this country gaining its independence we should be discussing a measure which a minority of this nation consider to be grossly oppressive. I am proud to consider myself a typical man of that minority. We against whom you have done this thing are no petty people. We are one of the great stocks of Europe. We are

---

*The precise amendment was the deletion of Article 44, Section 1 (ii and iii). In this chapter, however, I follow popular practice by referring to the deleted sub-sections simply as 'Article 44'.

the people of Burke; we are the people of Grattan; we are the people of Swift, the people of Emmet, the people of Parnell. We have created the most of the modern literature of this country. We have created the best of its political intelligence. Yet I do not altogether regret what has happened. I shall be able to find out, if not I, then my children will be able to find out whether we have lost our stamina or not. You have defined our position and have given us a popular following. If we have not lost our stamina, then your victory will be brief, and your defeat final, and when it comes this nation may be transformed.[6]

It was elegant, arrogant, aristocratic; it offended almost everybody. The very list of names which Yeats cited was enough to show that a unique man of genius was very far from being 'a typical man of that minority'. Yeats was a strange spokesman for the minority that had created Jacob's biscuits and Guinness's stout, Findlater's tea and Bewley's buns, the Boys' Brigade and the Adelaide Hospital Linen Guild. This was on the whole a community conservative both in manners and in morals. Yet Yeats did speak for it in a sense: it might not approve of divorce, but it felt much more strongly about the encroachment of the Catholic Church upon individual liberty. It was automatically in opposition to the attitude expressed by Senator William Magennis: 'You cannot be a good Catholic if you would allow divorce even between Protestants.'

The government's plan, however, ran into an uncharted rock. Lord Glenavy, Chairman of the Senate and a lawyer of distinction, ruled that the resolution was unconstitutional. The matter lapsed, therefore, until Mr de Valera's constitution of 1937, which introduced a positive prohibition upon divorce. The section in question (Article 41, Section 3) requires to be quoted in full; even the use of capital letters should be noted.

(i) The State pledges itself to guard with special care the institution of Marriage, on which the Family is founded, and to protect it against attack.

(ii) No law shall be enacted providing for the grant of a dissolution of marriage.

(iii) No person whose marriage has been dissolved under the civil law of any other State but is a subsisting valid

E

marriage under the law for the time being in force within the jurisdiction of the Government and Parliament established by this Constitution shall be capable of contracting a valid marriage within that jurisdiction during the lifetime of the other party to the marriage so dissolved.[7]

What the last section says, or appears to say, is that the man or woman who has secured a foreign divorce and remarries in the Republic will be guilty of bigamy. That is how the law stands in 1974; and since it is embodied in the constitution it cannot be changed without a referendum.

The question now arises: what happens if the state enacts a law which is not binding on the conscience of a section of the people? The answer is that that section of the people starts thinking of ways to evade the law. And the state is then on the horns of a dilemma, for it must either make nonsense of the law by permitting it to be disregarded, or it must render the law oppressive by enforcing it against people who are not bound in conscience. As the attitude to divorce has become more and more permissive throughout the western world, numbers of Irish people—Protestants and disobedient Catholics—have sought for ways to dissolve their marriages and remarry without being prosecuted for bigamy. The normal device is to establish domicile (real or fictitious) in Britain, and then to take advantage of the relatively liberal divorce procedures available in that country. In cases where this process is, for one reason or another, impracticable, the parties have secured divorce by flying to the United States or Mexico. Such techniques of escape are of course available only to those who can afford them, and the expense is often considerable. But they are now practised so frequently, and with such evidence of consent from society, that the constitutional prohibition has become a farce. Remarriage may—presumably does—involve bigamy, but the state prudently turns a blind eye.

* * *

Matters are further complicated by the fact that the Catholic Church does not recognise either civil marriage or civil divorce. In the eyes of the church a registry-office marriage is no marriage at all, and accordingly either partner remains free to marry again. On the other hand, a civil divorce does not nullify a church marriage, so a divorced person who remarries is held to be living in sin. But the church itself may grant a decree of nullity (and its judgment as to grounds for annulment has become very much broader and more humane within recent years) while a couple remain firmly bound in matrimony by the law of the state.

The clash between these codes was illustrated in 1945, when a Tipperary man, Robert Hunt, formally pleaded guilty to a charge of bigamy. Hunt, a Protestant, had been married in a London registry office to Martha Crotty, a Catholic. They had two children. When they returned to Ireland they lived apart, and Hunt contracted a liaison with one Rose McCarthy. In 1944 Hunt was received into the Catholic Church, and two days later he was married to Rose McCarthy by his parish priest, Canon O'Dwyer. It was stated in evidence that the priest had 'ascertained that the wife whom he had married at Holborn was a Catholic, and accordingly informed him that his first marriage was invalid and was not binding in the eyes of God or in the eyes of the church'. Canon O'Dwyer was fully aware that the second marriage was bigamous under civil law, but he had received specific approval from the Archbishop of Cashel. Mr Justice Lavery—who quoted Articles 42 and 44 of the constitution in his judgment—held that 'there had been a certain calculated intention to disobey the law of the land, but in the whole of the circumstances the case could not be regarded as a flagrant type of case'. He imposed a suspensory sentence of six months plus £75 costs.[8]

A good deal of indignation was aroused by this judgment, which appeared to indicate that the church could guarantee its adherents immunity against the penalties of the law. The state, it was argued, was effectively removing the protection of the law from the Protestant man or woman who might, in all good faith, go through a registry-office marriage with a Catholic, and might later be set aside in favour of another partner with the blessing of the church and the connivance of the state.

The Protestant churches accept the principle of divorce, but only as the lesser evil. Indeed, the Church of Ireland still rules that no divorced person may remarry with the rites of the church. The Presbyterian view perhaps reflects more accurately a contemporary Protestant position: 'Marriage involves at least two kinds of relationship, contractual and personal. Contractual relationships can be protected by law. Personal relationships cannot.'⁹

As we shall see, certain other restrictions on personal rights have been found unconstitutional in recent times by the Supreme Court. Such a recourse can scarcely be available against the constitution itself. There is no reason to suppose that any government will be eager to seek a change by referendum; and indeed, there could be no confidence that such a referendum could be carried. It seems probable that a change, if it is to come, will come only by way of a general revision in the constitution. Meanwhile Article 41.3 (ii) remains an anomaly in a constitution which no longer recognises the 'special position' of the Roman Catholic Church.

Contraception

While divorce is the concern of the constitution, the provisions relating to contraceptives are embodied in the criminal law. In 1973 a vast breach was made in a legal rampart which had stood for almost fifty years. Mrs Mary McGee, a Catholic wife and mother of Skerries, Co. Dublin, applied to the Supreme Court for a ruling that the law prohibiting the importation of contraceptives was unconstitutional. By a majority of four to one, the court decided in Mrs McGee's favour. By virtue of the court's decision the repugnant law was immediately annulled, and the importation of contraceptives became legal. Although the court was not asked for any ruling concerning the prohibition on sale of contraceptives, it was made clear that, if Mrs McGee experienced undue difficulty in securing the supplies she required, this provision might be pronounced unconstitutional also. Mrs McGee's legal victory brought to an issue the confusions and uncertainties of a situation which had lasted nearly half a century.

*   *   *

The law forbidding the sale or importation of contraceptives was introduced in 1925. It was reinforced by an amendment to the Censorship Act empowering the Censorship Board to ban any publication which advocated 'the unnatural prevention of conception'. In introducing these laws the government of the day was clearly following the dictates of Catholic morality. It is instructive to look back at the climate in which they were introduced.

The prohibition was embodied in the Criminal Law Amendment Act of 1925, the main purpose of which was to stiffen the penalties for certain classes of sexual offence, including assaults on idiot girls. Under Section 17 of the act it became unlawful for any person 'to sell, expose, offer, advertise, or keep for sale, or to import or attempt to import into Saorstát Éireann, for sale, any contraceptive'. The section would appear to leave it open to a citizen to import contraceptives for personal use, but this loophole was blocked by including contraceptives among the goods prohibited under the Customs Consolidation Act of 1876. The whole topic, it is clear, was regarded as shady. When Dr Rowlette, a member for Dublin University, came to speak on the matter in the Dáil, he did so in a tone of apology. He understood, he said, that 'the general moral judgment and feeling in this country is against any such practice', and with that judgment he found himself personally in agreement. He went on to make a plea for some leniency in the law, in the interests of married couples who suffered from transmissible physical ailments, and of wives whose health might be endangered by pregnancy. Nobody bothered to reply.[10]

The *Irish Times* expressed concern that the ban might encourage the spread of disease, increase the rate of illegitimacy and lead to more infanticide. A few correspondents commented on the measure; nearly all those who opposed it were anonymous. 'Vox Populi' thought it 'a flagrant encroachment on personal liberty', and 'Husband and Father' wrote: 'Whether they [Catholics] form 90 per cent of the population, or even more, they have no right to enforce their standards upon those of us who have equally strong moral convictions on the other side of the question.' He was answered by Margaret Gavan Duffy: 'If this is a Catholic country, it might well seem that Catholic moral standards might be enforced in it. But, waiving this question, one might be allowed to point out that the prevention of conception is against the standards of purely natural law, which, in this matter, is merely reinforced by the Church.' Since the church, however, was the guardian and exponent of the natural law, the distinction was a fine one.

'Husband and Father' probably expressed the view of most

Protestants, but there was no heat in the argument. Some Protestant churchmen tended to the Catholic viewpoint. Even those who spoke up for the right of birth control did so, as a rule, on the basis of hard cases. There was no reference to anything so frivolous as love. The whole subject was invested with an air of impropriety, and the name of Marie Stopes conjured up an aura of unimaginable sin. Since the Censorship Board used its powers to ban all publications advocating 'Birth Control and Race Suicide', open debate on the subject was almost out of the question. Only one side of the case might be heard; the other was silenced. In 1954 Paul Blanshard claimed that

> The Catholic doctors' associations dare not resist or expose the ignorance of the priests. Nowhere in the Republic could any young Irish person discover for himself that his nation stands alone among English-speaking countries in its position on birth control, and that the overwhelming majority of people in the West accept contraception as a respectable practice.[11]

All this does not mean, of course, that nobody used contraceptives; but they had to be smuggled into the country under the risk—however slight—of prosecution. In fact, people who defended the law quite commonly argued that it could not be construed as unfair to Protestants, since they could always buy their packets of Durex on a day-trip to Belfast.

A change of attitude became evident in the 1960s. It was part of the wave of new thinking that swept Ireland during that decade; but in the case of birth control there was one very special cause, and that was the introduction of the contraceptive pill. For many Catholics this raised a new question. Was it permissible or was it not? They looked to the Vatican for a ruling; and while the Pope delayed, thousands of them anticipated his decision. Doctors began to prescribe the pill more or less openly, on the pretext that it was to control menstruation. Chemists sold it on prescription over the counter. When the ruling eventually came, in the encyclical *Humanae Vitae*, it declared the pill as a contraceptive to be unlawful. But by this time a large number of people had made their own decision, and they were prepared to back the ruling of conscience against the ruling of the Pope.

In the following years family planning became an open subject. It was debated freely and often on television. Family planning clinics operated openly and under the most reputable medical authority; in 1973 they claimed to have had 10,000 consultations within the past two years, and to have fitted 2,700 intra-uterine devices. The state, having a bad law on its hands, closed its eyes and allowed the law to be broken. But laws are not less oppressive in principle because they are not enforced. Mrs Mary Robinson, a dynamic young lawyer who held a Dublin University seat in the Senate, introduced a private bill to change the law. Then, while public feet were being shuffled, a vigilant customs officer intercepted in the post a contraceptive device addressed to Mrs Mary McGee.

* * *

In May 1972 Mrs McGee went to the High Court seeking a declaration that the law forbidding her to import the device was repugnant to the constitution. Her evidence was that her health would be endangered by another pregnancy and that the pill did not suit her. Her only hope of maintaining normal marital relations with her husband was to use a contraceptive. The High Court turned down her application and she appealed to the Supreme Court.

While the reserved judgment of the court was awaited the Catholic hierarchy issued a statement of its own position. The clear teaching of the church, they said, was that artificial contraception was morally wrong; but they went on:

> It does not follow, of course, that the State is bound to prohibit the importation and sale of contraceptives. There are many things which the Catholic Church holds to be morally wrong and which nobody has ever suggested, least of all the Church herself, that they should be prohibited by the State.

The bishops went on to relate the sale of contraceptives to increases in illegitimacy and abortion, and to refer to 'the corrosive effect on the very concepts of marriage and the family which this contraceptive mentality has had in some Western societies'; but they said in their conclusion:

> We emphasise that it is not a matter for bishops to decide whether the law should be changed or not. That is a matter

for the legislators after a conscientious consideration of all the factors involved.[12]

The bishops' statement admitted at least the possibility of dissent, and in this it marked a distinct change from the climate of 1951.

The next act belonged, however, to Mrs McGee. In December the Supreme Court brought in its judgment upholding her appeal. In the words of Mr Justice Walsh, delivering an historic judgment,

> The private morality of the citizens does not justify intervention by the State into the activities of those citizens unless and until the common good requires it.[13]

The ruling meant that contraceptives might be imported by anybody, in any quantity, without hindrance. The prohibitions on sale and advertising and the provisions of the Censorship of Publications Act were not directly affected. It was clear, however, that the state must face the problem of redrafting the law. This task fell to Mr Patrick Cooney, Minister for Justice, in the coalition government which took office in January 1973 under Mr Liam Cosgrave.

The new bill was introduced to the Dáil in June 1974. It was, at the best, an uneasy compromise. It provided that contraceptives might be sold legally, but only by special suppliers and only to married couples. Most advocates of reform believed the restrictions to be undesirable in principle, and unenforceable in practice. The issue was brought to the Dáil, with Fianna Fáil committed to oppose it, and government members permitted a free vote. In the division lobby it was defeated, by 75 votes to 61; and astonished deputies on the government benches saw their own leader, Mr Cosgrave, with one of his ministers, walk into the 'No' lobby with the opposition.

For the time being, then—and in default of any further judgments by the Supreme Court—the law would remain as it was. There was some life still in the concept of 'the Catholic nation'.

The Special Position

Throughout the 1930s Catholic social teaching was being

absorbed into the thinking of the state. This process reached its formal culmination with Mr de Valera's new constitution of 1937. The primary motive of this exercise was, of course, republican rather than Catholic. But the constitution also set out to restate certain social principles, and in doing so it brought all such rights under the broad umbrella of Christian belief.

Religious freedom had been guaranteed by the constitution of 1922 in one workmanlike clause. Article 44 restated all such guarantees, but it preceded them by a new set of declarations:

(i) The State acknowledges that the homage of public worship is due to Almighty God. It shall hold His Name in reverence, and shall respect and honour religion.

(ii) The State recognises the special position of the Holy Catholic Apostolic and Roman Church as the guardian of the Faith professed by the great majority of the citizens.

(iii) The State also recognises the Church of Ireland, the Presbyterian Church in Ireland, the Methodist Church in Ireland, the Religious Society of Friends in Ireland, as well as the Jewish Congregations and the other religious denominations existing in Ireland at the date of the coming into operation of this Constitution.[14]

It must be said at once that Protestants made little or no objection to this article. It was reported in fact that Archbishop Gregg had been consulted about the correct titles of the various churches. In the Dáil the main criticism came from Mr Frank MacDermot. He moved the deletion of the 'special position' on the ground that it meant nothing: 'It seemed to serve no purpose except to create misunderstanding.' Mr de Valera said that no objections had been put forward by the other churches, and the amendment was withdrawn.[15] Until some practical effects appeared, the minority was not disposed to fuss about a clause which appeared to be no more than a formal nod in the direction of the Catholic nation.

* * *

Article 44 did not herald any change of direction by the state; but it did provide the basis for certain new interpretations of the law. The author of these precedents was Mr Justice

Gavan Duffy of the High Court. The trend of the judge's thinking was revealed in 1945, when he ruled that a priest was entitled to claim privilege in court for communications made to him in the confessional. The judge thus set aside an established principle of common law by reference to the constitution:

> That Constitution in express terms recognises the special position amongst us of the Holy Catholic Apostolic and Roman Church as the guardian of the Faith professed by the great majority of the citizens, and that recognition is solemn and deliberate. . . .
>
> In a State where nine out of every ten citizens today are Catholics, and on a matter closely touching the religious outlook of the people, it would be intolerable that the common law, as expounded after the Reformation in a Protestant land, should be taken to bind a nation which persistently repudiated the Reformation as heresy.[16]

There was a point here: the Irish people had never had the opportunity to develop their own legal system, and the common law had been taken over part and parcel from England. Still, taken together with the judgment in the Hunt case (in the same year), this ruling seemed to grant Catholic clergy a status above the civil law.

A good deal more concern was caused by the ruling of the same judge (then President of the High Court) in 1950, in the marital dispute which is known as the Tilson case. Here the law intervened in the most sensitive area of inter-church relations—the mixed marriage. Mr Ernest Tilson, a Protestant, had married Mary Josephine Barnes, a Catholic, when she was only sixteen. He had signed the undertaking required by the Catholic Church that he would permit the children of the marriage to be baptised and brought up as Catholics. Subsequently he changed his mind, and he removed three of the four children from his wife's home to a Protestant orphanage. Mrs Tilson applied to the court for custody of her children.

Nobody was much concerned to defend Mr Tilson's conduct as a husband and father or as a man of his word; but he appeared to have acted within his legal rights as sole head of the family. The question before the court was whether the promise given before marriage could be treated as a legally enforceable contract. The judge held that there was under Irish law no injustice, no impropriety and no denial of first principles in holding a man to his pledge:

> In my opinion, an order of the Court designed to secure the fulfilment of an agreement, peremptorily required before a 'mixed marriage' by the Church whose special position in Ireland is officially recognised as the guardian of the Catholic spouse, cannot be withheld on any ground of public policy by the very State which pays that homage to that Church.[17]

The judge ruled that the ante-nuptial undertaking had binding force, and he made an order that the children should be returned to their mother. The Supreme Court, on appeal, upheld the judgment by a majority of four to one. The dissenting judge, it was instantly noticed, was the only Protestant on the bench.

The Supreme Court based its decision entirely on its reading of Article 42, which set out the rights and duties of parents. Of Articles 41 and 44 it said: 'The Court, in arriving at its decision, is not now holding that these last-mentioned Articles confer any privileged status before the law upon members of the Roman Catholic Church.' This reservation did little to soothe the feelings of Protestants. The attitude of the Catholic Church in relation to mixed marriages was already widely resented as arrogant and overbearing. It now appeared that the power of the state would back the ruling of the church. 'It is difficult', said the *Irish Times,* 'to avoid the impression that the philosophy underlying Irish jurisprudence is tending, slowly but surely, to be informed by the principles of the Roman Catholic Church.'[18]

* * *

But the concern of five per cent is really no more than a minor irritant to the body politic. And, indeed, it must be admitted that there was no spate of judgments calculated to follow these precedents and to extend the effect of Article 44 as a guiding principle in the law of the state. The matter therefore rested fairly easily until the dawn of the 1970s.

Mention has already been made of the new wave of thinking that spread over Ireland in the 1960s. A vital element in that new thinking was the spirit of ecumenism, or, in plain words, of fellowship between Christians. The Second Vatican Council gave the opportunity for a revaluation of the relationship between Catholics and Christians of other churches. But the impetus came, in Ireland, from the wave of violence which broke out in the North after 1969. It was this which made Irish Catholics in general, and Irish politicians in particular, look seriously at the obstacles to unity between the two segments of their country. They saw that one obstacle was the 'special position' of the Catholic Church. It was a symbolic obstacle, of course, not a real one; but symbols are not unimportant in this context. Almost overnight the idea of removing Article 44 became a matter of current politics.

When Mr Jack Lynch's Fianna Fáil government took up the issue in 1972 they must have been astonished to meet so little opposition. Of course some conservative clergy were against a change; but Cardinal Conway said he 'would not shed a tear'. The opposition declined to oppose. A public meeting called in Dublin to 'Defend 44' attracted a couple of hundred people. In December 1972 the people were asked by referendum to delete Article 44, and the proposal was carried with a majority of 84 per cent of the poll.

Inevitably the government's action produced some cynical comments. In the North earnest Unionists saw it as a sop, and poured scorn on Mr Lynch for thinking that he could woo them by so transparent a device. But it would be wrong to underestimate the sincerity of the motives that led to the death of Article 44 and the end of the 'special position'. They were rooted, in the end, in the ordinary Irishman's deep-seated belief in the rights of the individual.

Erosion by Marriage

THERE is no single cause that contributes so much to the embitterment of inter-faith relations as the rule of the Roman Catholic Church concerning mixed marriages. In any circle of Protestants, of any age-group, in any part of the country, this is the first reason that will be advanced to justify segregation in education and in social activities. Protestant parents do not want their children to mix with Catholics because they may marry Catholics; and if they marry Catholics, then the church will insist on an undertaking that the children of the marriage shall be brought up Catholics. Moreover, by the precedent of the Tilson case, once such an undertaking has been given it may be enforced by the law of the land. As Protestants see it, their children are being placed in a situation of emotional blackmail, in which the price of love is the sacrifice of their own convictions. This is the situation which a Church of Ireland bishop has described as 'inhuman and immoral'.

Among younger people there is, of course, a growing indifference to religion. They may be angered or amused by the scruples of their parents. What, they may ask, does it matter? The only answer is that it matters to some people. A Protestant woman brought up in Co. Donegal some thirty years ago told me: 'My parents would have preferred to see me come home with an illegitimate baby than with a Catholic husband.'

There is much more to this, of course, than a simple resistance to the doctrine of Rome. There is at least a vestige of the old snobbery: Catholics, in the colonial ethos, are socially inferior persons. But much more potent today is the sense of threat to the survival of the community. Among older people, at any rate, this is accompanied by a resentment against a Catholic Church which is seen to be aggressive and grasping: a kind of ecclesiastical press-gang, on the alert to haul aboard any Protestant who may be weakened by isolation, illness, or the disease of love. Some believe that a Catholic girl gets good marks from the priest if she can hook a Protestant and make him 'turn'.

The threat to survival is very real. Dr Brendan Walsh's figures indicate that in 1961 as many as three out of every ten Protestant grooms and two out of every ten Protestant brides married Catholics. (See pages 13-15.) The figures are probably higher year by year; and a mixed marriage in this generation must mean—if the rule of the church is obeyed—an all-Catholic family in the next. In a shrinking community, warnings and exhortations are of no avail. The process of intermarriage continues, and with it the leaching away of the Protestant community.

* * *

It is fruitless to explore this subject unless one accepts that it involves a matter of conscience for members of the Roman Catholic Church. In the words of Dr Daly, Bishop of Ardagh, 'We are anxious to do everything that conscience allows, in dialogue and in co-operation with other Churches, to make the problems of mixed marriages less hurtful to relations between the Churches and less painful for the partners of inter-Church marriages.'[1] But fundamentally the Catholic Church holds that a Catholic parent has an obligation to pass on the faith to his or her children, and that this obligation is imposed by the law of God, and accordingly may be interpreted, but not varied, by the law of the church.

Intermarriage between Protestant and Catholic has always taken place, of course, in spite of the ferocious penalties prescribed under the penal laws. In some cases the parents, by agreement, applied the 'Palatine pact'—that is, the girls took the religion of the mother, the boys the religion of the father. Such marriages were looked on with disfavour by the church— a bishop's letter of 1780 describes them as 'unlawful, wicked and dangerous'—but they were admitted to be canonically valid. It was not until the middle of the last century that the church was strong enough to lay down firm conditions: mixed marriages were permitted only subject to a dispensation from Rome, and there could be no dispensation from the obligation to bring up the children in the Catholic faith. In 1908, by the *Ne Temere* decree, specific conditions were laid down for the issue of a dispensation. These were embodied in the Code of Canon Law in 1918. Substantial changes were made following the Second Vatican Council, and these new laws, set out in the apostolic letter *Motu Proprio*, now govern the situation.

The decree *Ne Temere* was primarily concerned with laying down the conditions for canonical marriage between Catholics, and it was only as a side-issue that it went into the regulations for mixed marriages. Basically it prescribed that, as a condition of a dispensation, both parties must give undertakings that all the children of the marriage would be brought up in the Catholic Church. The undertakings were normally, but not necessarily, given in writing. The authority competent to give a dispensation was the bishop of the diocese, and at the same time he had the right to lay down the conditions under which the marriage might be performed. In the Dublin diocese, under Archbishop McQuaid, the ruling was that no wedding could take place during mass; in general the ceremony had to be performed before 9 a.m., and it had to take place in the sacristy, not in the church proper. Much resentment was caused by the archbishop's insistence on this furtive ritual.

* * *

The Second Vatican Council took a new approach to the relationship between the Christian churches: it held that there was still only one true church, but it also recognised that other Christians shared, albeit imperfectly, in the truth of Christ. It was appropriate therefore that the Holy Office should take a new look at the problem of mixed marriages. The result was a new code, set out in 1970 in the apostolic letter *Motu Proprio*. It must be said that in tone and language it is humane and tolerant, and the regulations which it lays down mark a real and substantial advance on the terms of *Ne Temere*.

The new ruling is that a bishop may grant a dispensation for a marriage between a Catholic and a non-Catholic 'provided there is a just cause'. In order to obtain a dispensation the Catholic party

shall declare that he is ready to remove dangers of falling away from the faith. He is also gravely bound to make a sincere promise to do all in his power to have all the children baptised and brought up in the Catholic Church.[2]

The non-Catholic partner is not required to give any undertakings whatsoever. However, he (or she) is to be informed of the promise made by the Catholic partner, 'so that it is clear that he is cognisant of the promise and obligation on the part of the Catholic'.

The bishop is also given the right, 'if serious difficulties stand in the way', to dispense with the normal canonical form of marriage. He may therefore give permission to have the marriage celebrated in a Protestant church and by a Protestant minister. At such a ceremony it is considered desirable that a Catholic priest should attend, although the letter specifically forbids a joint celebration of the marriage.

The letter finally lays on the bishops and the parish priests a positive duty concerning pastoral care of the married couple and their family:

> They shall encourage the Catholic husband or wife to keep ever in mind the divine gift of the Catholic faith and to bear witness to it with gentleness and reverence, and with a clear conscience. They are to aid the married couple to foster the unity of their conjugal and family life, a unity which, in the case of Christians, is based on their baptism too. To these ends it is to be desired that these pastors should establish relationships of sincere openness and enlightened confidence with ministers of other religious groups.

The implications of this last section—suggesting as it does that the clergy of both denominations undertake the duty of pastoral care in a spirit of partnership—are very profound indeed.

Motu Proprio leaves a wide discretion to the bishops; and it must be said that, in the view of many of their own communion, the Catholic bishops of Ireland have been excessively cautious in their application of the new rules. At an International Consultation on Mixed Marriages held in Dublin in September 1974 a Jesuit speaker contrasted the attitude of the Irish bishops with that of the bishops of Switzerland and other European countries:

One might say that, wherever special needs have made

themselves felt, the bishops have been most ready to avail themselves of the latitude afforded by the Vatican. . . . In Ireland, where the need for visible inter-church fellowship has been most acute, we have seen perhaps the least liberal implementation of the Papal Instruction.[3]

The problem, of course, may look rather different from the opposite points of view. To the Catholic Church in Ireland mixed marriages are still a relatively rare phenomenon. In the archdiocese of Dublin there were over 7,400 marriages in all during 1972, and only 388 of these involved a partner of another church. The Protestant clergy, on the other hand, are rather in the position of Canute confronting the waves. In an address to the same conference the Minister for Foreign Affairs of the Republic, Dr Garret FitzGerald, argued that the position taken by the Catholic Church on mixed marriages had contributed not only to the divisions within the North, but also to the Ulster Protestant's deep-rooted fear of closer association with the South:

> Protestants in Northern Ireland have observed a continuous decline in the number of their co-religionists in the Republic and . . . they have not attributed this decline in Protestant numbers in the Republic to mixed marriages but have instead assumed some other more sinister force had been at work. . . . The simple fact is that the fidelity of Roman Catholics to their church's teaching is so great in Ireland that even the simple maintenance of an obligation on the Roman Catholic partner to do his or her best to bring up the children as Roman Catholics imposes a major demographic distortion on the Republic, which has most dangerous consequences for Roman Catholics in Northern Ireland.
>
> The solution to this and to other similar ecclesiastical problems that is often found in other countries—viz., not to take the obligation too seriously—is ruled out in Ireland by the character of the religious observance of Irish Roman Catholics.[4]

In 1973 the Catholic bishops agreed to set up a joint working party with leaders of the major Protestant churches, to review the problem. Their concern, however, would not appear to be infused by any sense of urgency. In the words of the same Jesuit speaker, 'It is not good enough for our church leaders to act as though they believed time to be the greatest healer.'

Adoption

While the law admits of no discrimination between citizens on the grounds of religion, there is one group of citizens which has been the object of discrimination for twenty years, on what one can only call religious grounds. Under the Adoption Act of 1952, which introduced legal adoption to Ireland, couples who had made mixed marriages were prohibited from adopting children. Under the same act no child of a mixed marriage was eligible for adoption.

Before considering this anomalous provision of the law it is well to remind oneself that no form of legal adoption existed in the Irish state before 1952. In a period of just over twenty years it has become an institution so respected and so familiar that one can only look back with astonishment at the long-drawn-out action that was fought against it. The sword and buckler were wielded by successive Ministers for Justice. The influence behind them, without a doubt, was the Catholic Church. General Seán Mac Eóin—a fearless warrior of the fight against the British—explained his reluctance to tackle the matter in a phrase that went down to history as the epitaph of his government: 'I don't want to get a belt of a crozier.'

When Fianna Fáil returned to office in 1951 the matter was reactivated by a private member's bill (with support from both sides of the House). The minister, however, was prudent enough not to commit himself until a special committee of the Catholic hierarchy had reported its views. The committee concluded that adoption was acceptable in principle, subject to certain safeguards. All the safeguards were embodied in the act which became law in the following year.*

In order to safeguard the 'natural right and obligation' of parents, adoption was limited to children who were illegitimate or full orphans, aged between six months and seven years. The law required that the adoptive parents must be of the same

---

* Amendments were made in 1964 but not in the provisions which concern this chapter.

religion as the natural parents of the child, or, if the child was born out of wedlock, of the same religion as the mother. Since it is evident that adoptive parents of mixed religions could not *both* be of the same religion as the natural parents of the child, and that a child born of mixed parents could not be of the same religion as *both* his adoptive parents, the law simply provided no procedure whatever for adoption in these cases.

Responsibility for issuing adoption orders is vested in the Adoption Board, which is nominated by the Minister for Justice. It has a District Justice as chairman and two of the six members normally are Protestants. In 1973 the board issued 1,402 adoption orders. Cases are brought before the board either by voluntary adoption societies (almost all of which are denominational bodies maintained by private subscription) or by local authorities.

The Protestant Adoption Society, which is affiliated to all the Protestant churches, placed forty-eight children in 1973— all, of course, with Protestant couples. (For the purposes of the law Protestant and Catholic are different religions, but there is no difference between, say, Anglican and Methodist.) Since there is always a waiting list of prospective parents, the Society is able to be fairly exacting in its requirements. So long as they can provide a suitable home, the income-group of the adopting couple is not a factor. If one partner has been divorced, this may be a factor in assessing the suitability of the adopters, but it is not a bar.

Overall the system works pretty well. The Society has placed over seven hundred children since 1952; there must be a percentage of errors, but it is impossible to estimate—once an order for adoption has been made it is absolute, and neither the Adoption Board nor the Protestant Adoption Society has any right of review. Criticisms to date have turned mainly on inadequate inspection of prospective adopters. More professional social workers are needed, and the state will have to provide the funds, since the societies, quite properly, take no fees for their services.

In 1974, however, a Dublin couple attacked a much more fundamental fault in the system. Mr and Mrs X (their names were not disclosed in court) were of different religions: Mr X was Irish and a Catholic, Mrs X a member of the Church of England. Mrs X had a child born out of wedlock by another man. The child was baptised in the Church of England. Since their marriage Mr and Mrs X were bringing up the child as their own (in the Catholic faith), and they had applied to the Adoption Board to adopt him legally. The board, in accordance with the Adoption Act, was obliged to reject the application. Mrs X, in short, was refused leave to adopt her own son.

Mr and Mrs X brought the matter to the High Court, seeking a declaration that the decision of the board was unconstitutional. Mr Justice Pringle, giving judgment, declared the relevant section of the act (which, by construction, denied the right of adoption to couples of mixed religion) to be repugnant to Article 44.2 (iii) of the constitution, which states:

> The State shall not impose any disabilities or make any discrimination on the ground of religious profession, belief or status.[4]

The decision of the court automatically placed couples of mixed religion (and presumably the orphan children of such couples) on an equal footing with all other citizens in respect of adoption.

Footnote

The attentive reader of Chapters 10 and 11 may have observed what appears to be a changing trend in the decisions of Irish courts. In the decade up to 1951 the judgments of Mr Justice Gavan Duffy had given rise to the comment that 'Irish jurisprudence is tending, slowly but surely, to be informed by the principles of the Roman Catholic Church.' In the 1970s the judgments of the High Court in the matter of adoption and of the Supreme Court in the matter of contraception appear, on the contrary, to have thrown the emphasis back upon the protection of personal rights. Lawyers may consider that this new trend has arisen from the deletion of Article 44.1, which recognised 'the special position' of the Roman Catholic Church, and which might have been construed to override the more general guarantees of religious equality. If this is the case, the deletion of that part of the article will be seen to have had very much more than symbolic significance.

Education: Sheep and Other Sheep

T H E child stands at the end of a rough boreen, where it opens on to the tarred road across the bleak brown back of a Donegal mountain. At 8.50 a.m. every morning a yellow minibus comes spinning up the road, stops for a minute to pick him up, and is off again: passing the boarded-up shell of Meenacahan National School, where his father and his brothers—as likely as not—went to school: stopping at other crosses and gaps and gates to pick up other children; bringing them all down six or eight or ten miles towards Glenties, to sit in class with thirty or forty other children gathered in from the mountainsides. At three o'clock the minibus will be waiting to bring them home again.

Somebody has said that the school bus is the symbol of the new Ireland. But it is a little hard to say exactly what it symbolises. Compromise, perhaps: compromise between the principle of educational equality and the hard facts of economics. A generation ago a handful of children would have trudged down to Meenacahan to learn their sums and their spellings from a single teacher. Bring the children together into larger units and you can give them better buildings, better facilities, more teachers, a broader curriculum. And it costs less. This is rationalisation, and it is very hard to argue against it.

But rationalisation is not strictly rational. If there happens to be a little Protestant boy up there at Meenacahan, another bus will go to collect him. And it will bring him perhaps twice as far, to a national school under the management of a Protestant minister, where he will be able to sit in class with other little Protestants, and be taught his sums and his spellings by a Protestant teacher. And at three o'clock the Protestant bus will be waiting outside the school to bring him home again.

If a school bus symbolises the new Ireland, what does a Protestant school bus symbolise?

* * *

The Irish national system of education that evolved in the nineteenth century has been preserved, as if in amber, in the Irish Republic's schools of the twentieth century. The system remained unchanged until after independence. Thereafter, the connection between the systems of primary and secondary education was clearly articulated so that a child could go from one to the other without inconvenience, but there reform stopped. The schools now inculcate Irish patriotism instead of British history, and drum the Irish language into the heads of Irish children. But structurally little has changed. To this day Irish primary schools remain small, clerically-managed institutions, in which Roman Catholic rarely meets Protestant. Primary and secondary education remain distinct, and secondary education is not compulsory. Advanced as the Irish national system may have been for the first half of the nineteenth century, it is a brittle fossil in the second half of the twentieth.[1]

In this trenchant paragraph an historian of Irish education has summed up the record of almost a century and a half. The educational system inherited by the Irish Free State was a system of state support for denominational schools. But this system had evolved, under pressure from the churches, from the brave attempt of ninety years earlier to establish 'a system of education from which should be banished for ever even the suspicion of proselytism, and which, admitting children of all religious persuasions, should not interfere with the peculiar tenets of any'.[2] In an era of evangelical zeal this respect for the beliefs of others was an example of rare enlightenment. It did not stand up for long against the pressure of the churches. The Presbyterians were the first to kick: they did not intend to share with papists. By stubborn pugnacity they hammered out enough concessions to ensure that they would have denominational control in their schools, while holding on to their share of the public money that went to provide teachers, buildings and books.

The Anglicans, who considered it the prerogative of the Established Church to superintend education for everybody, withdrew from the system and set up their own schools. The Catholics welcomed the state system at first, but after 1850, when they had more money and fewer people, the bishops exerted their new power to secure control. By the middle of the century 'the national system had become a denominational system. Throughout the system, Catholic children were taught in schools normally run by a Catholic manager (usually the parish priest) and staffed solely by Catholic teachers. Protestant children were taught in Protestant schools managed by the local parson or landlord and staffed solely by Protestants.'[3] In its essentials, this system was handed on unaltered to the first government of the Free State.

In spite of all the in-fighting, the national school system made an inestimable contribution to the advancement of the Irish people. In the sixty years from 1841 to 1901 the number of primary pupils went up from 475,559 to 636,777, though the total population was almost halved in the same period; and the proportion who could neither read nor write fell from over 50 per cent to 14 per cent.

* * *

The moral tone of the national schools was the tone of Victorian Christianity—Reformed or Roman according to choice. Religion apart, the curriculum was strictly utilitarian. There was no recognition of the Irish as a separate nationality.

The national factor in Ireland has been studiously eliminated from national education [wrote Horace Plunkett], and Ireland is perhaps the only country in Europe where it was part of the settled policy of those who had the guidance of education to ignore the literature, history, arts and traditions of the people. It was a fatal policy, for it obviously tended to stamp their native country in the eyes of Irishmen with the badge of inferiority.[4]

Given the close links between the language revival and the Sinn Féin movement, it was inevitable that the new state would see the revival of Irish as one of its responsibilities. From 1922 onwards the language was given a central place in the national schools, and it became an essential subject for Intermediate and Leaving Certificate examinations. Protestant educators in general had little sympathy with this development. They were faced with great difficulty in finding qualified teachers, and the standard of teaching was frequently low. The Primate made conciliatory noises, and the Bishop of Tuam earnestly sought 'to get rid of any idea that they were opposed to compulsory Irish for sectarian reasons'.⁵ But the parents were no doubt quoted correctly by the headmaster of the High School, Dublin: 'Of course, if the parents wish their children to learn modern Irish, we shall provide the facilities, but our experience is that not only do a large majority of parents not wish it, but on the contrary most of them decidedly object.'

The *Catholic Bulletin* had no difficulty in recognising that opposition to the language sprang from its old enemies, the Cromwellians: 'What they seek is to dictate the whole educational and cultural policy of the Irish people, on the lines and principles of the Ascendancy.' This was not quite fair. Protestants were concerned only for their own schools and their own children. They feared that educational standards would be depressed by this unwelcome burden, and that the language test would be a subtle barrier cutting off Protestant applicants from public appointments. 'One has really nothing to complain of', said the Dublin correspondent of *The Times*, 'if the authorities insist on Irish history and antiquities being an integral part of the school programme, but on educational grounds nothing has yet been said justifying forcing upon children a study whose value is almost wholly philological.'⁶

With the exception of this one issue it has never been suggested that the state was unfair or discriminatory in its dealings with Protestant education. In recent years the basic problem has been common to all: how to meet a demand for higher standards in an era of rising costs. It is becoming increasingly evident that, for a small and widely dispersed minority, separate control of schools presents problems which it may be beyond the capacity of that minority to solve. We must now try to look at some of those problems in the context of the educational policy of the Republic in the 1970s.

* * *

There are rather more than half a million children in primary schools in the Republic, of whom 12,769 are of the three main

Protestant denominations.* Most of them are in small schools of one or two teachers. Nearly all the schools are Church of Ireland property (the Presbyterians have a sprinkling of schools in the Ulster counties and the Methodists have two or three in Dublin). In nearly every case the school manager is the local rector. In effect, then, the schools are parish schools.

The key figure in this set-up is the manager. He is responsible for the administration of the school—for heating, lighting, routine maintenance. The Department of Education gives a grant towards these charges but the balance is borne by the parish. If a new classroom is needed, or a whole new school, the department may give a grant ranging from two-thirds of the cost to five-sixths or even more; but the parish must find the balance and is legally responsible for the debt. Teachers are paid by the department, but the manager has the sole right of appointment and dismissal: the principal teacher has no written-in right to participate in the selection of his staff, and there have been cases in which the manager did not even consult the principal because 'it was none of his business'. The manager has control over admissions to the school, though the enrolment of the pupils and their assignment to classes are the responsibility of the principal. The same regulations, of course, apply to all national schools, whether under the management of Roman Catholics, Anglicans, Presbyterians or Jews.

In a system so heavily loaded in favour of the amateur manager, as against the professional teacher, it is easy to see that frictions can develop. The Department of Education would say that the manager represents the parish, which has contributed, probably for generations, to maintaining the school, and still bears quite a heavy financial responsibilty. There is, however, no right of representation at all for a group who might be considered the most deeply concerned of all—the parents.

In today's terms, both building and maintenance costs may outstrip the means of a small parish. The economics of education obviously tend towards larger units. For the scattered Protestants in the rural areas—perhaps no more than one or two per cent—even amalgamation of schools would appear to have its physical limits. What then? Integration?

* Figures for 1970: the Department of Education can give no breakdown by religion for later years.

The Department of Education, though perforce on the side of the larger school, has done its best to be fair to the minority of separatists. A school will be allowed to stay open with as few as seven children on the roll, and in fact it may not be obliged to close until the number has fallen below this level for two or more years. Some educationalists would argue that a small school like this has its own special qualities, in that it reproduces something like the environment of the family. But the buildings are generally old and dilapidated, and the bright young teachers—unless they have special ties with the locality—will want the community of a larger school, and work that falls more readily within the normal definition of education.

As the Protestant community dwindles, the small school must close, and the pupils must take the school bus each morning to go to a larger centre: nine from Drum will drive to join ten from Inish; nine from Drum and ten from Inish will drive to join eleven from Kill; and so on, and so on, and so on. In the end you may have children ferried fifty miles or more daily—leaving home at seven in the morning and coming back at seven at night—for the sake of sitting in class with others of their own religion. Is the price of segregation—in fatigue, in destruction of home life, as well as in expense—too high to pay? If the nine little Protestants of Drum walk a mile or two down the road to go to school with 150 little Catholics, will anybody be worse off?

A number of parents have already made up their own minds. In rural areas, where Protestants are scarce, some of the children go to Catholic schools. Under the department's rules, the clergy of their own church must have access to the school in such cases, to give them religious instruction. I have heard of no case in which a Catholic manager made any difficulty about observing this condition, though the facilities available are sometimes less than adequate (I have heard of one rector in the south-west who has to give his religious instruction class in the cloakroom for want of any other accommodation).

There is, nevertheless, a problem of identity. By gathering children together from ever-widening circles into a Protestant school, one can preserve for them some sense of a Protestant community. By sending them to a Catholic school in their own townland one can preserve a stronger link with their locality and a stronger tie with the home, while gaining the benefit of a larger unit. But a handful of Protestant children dispersed through all the classes of a Catholic school may be liable—with no ill-will on anybody's part—to feel themselves swamped, their sense of identity obliterated. Even in vocational schools, which are ouside the denominational system, the Protestant child may find himself confronted by the kind of symbols—a crucifix, a holy picture, a statue of the Sacred Heart—which will make him feel alien.

* * *

The situation in Dublin is rather different. There, integration seems to be beginning from the other end: Catholic children are enrolling in Protestant schools. The number (in the suburban areas anyway) depends a good deal on the individual attitude of the school manager. One rector says that a quarter of his pupils are Catholics; another has only six on a roll of 120; a principal teacher says he could enrol as many as he is willing to take. The reasons for this trend are complex. Obviously it has something to do with a breaking down of religious barriers, a growing confidence that contact does not mean contamination. Added to this there may be a growing anticlericalism among educated Catholics. But the overriding reason is simply social. Protestants are fewer in number, so their schools are less crowded. Protestants are mostly middle-class, so they are not likely to infect their classmates with a 'gutty' accent. In a backhanded way the Protestants have acquired a position of privilege: religious segregation gives them the right to class segregation within a state system. It is hardly surprising that some Catholics in the same bracket of affluence want to share the privilege of being a minority.

Under the department's regulations a national school manager is bound to admit any applicant, provided a place is available. There is no provision for a religious test. On the other hand, the job of the managers—as they see it—is to provide a service for their own people. They use their own system of priorities to ensure that the child of a parishioner is never kept out because all the places have been taken by Catholics. But the whole system is based, really, on an identification of *parents* with *parishioners*. This holds good in the country but not in the city.

Where parents and principal are pulling one way, and rector and parish the other, the conflict may produce cracks in the whole structure. This is, in outline, what happened in the *cause célèbre* of Dalkey School.

* * *

Dalkey a hundred years ago was a fishing village a few miles from Dublin, the nucleus of a settlement of middle-class commuters who travelled to town every day by the railway. The parish school was built by a private endowment in the grounds of St Patrick's Church, and in 1891 became part of the national system.[7] In fifty years, from 1894 to 1944, only eighteen children not of the Church of Ireland appear in its rolls.

From 1960 to 1970 the pattern of enrolment showed a remarkable change. In 1960 seventeen children were admitted, and of these fourteen were of the Church of Ireland. In 1970 fifty-six children were admitted : the Church of Ireland number had gone up marginally, to seventeen, but the 'others' had shot up to thirty-nine. This rapid growth was due to the build-up of new housing in the area and the influx of Catholics of the professional class—managers, executives, university lecturers—who wanted their children to have free education in a national school but not in a *Catholic* school. But the special attraction was the reputation built up by the school under an outstandingly active and progressive principal.

The increase in numbers demanded new building, and, according to the usual system, a substantial share of the cost fell on the parish. By now many of the parents lived outside the parish, and many of those from within the area were not members of the Church of Ireland. The select vestry felt it was unfair that the burden of servicing a debt and paying heating, lighting and maintenance costs should fall on the parishioners alone. The parents formed an association to contribute to these expenses. There is some argument on both sides as to whether the burden was equitably shared. But what seems beyond doubt is that from this time onwards (about 1968) the parents felt that they had a share in the *running* of the school. On the other hand, the vestry felt that the rector, representing the parish, was gradually being ousted from his rightful position of control.

A dichotomy was developing, in short, between those who saw the school as a *parish* school and those who saw it as a *national* school. The Parent-Teacher Association wanted to push ahead to a multi-denominational school of perhaps three hundred pupils, with eight teachers and a high level of accommodation and facilities. The vestry, well aware that a majority of parishioners were beyond the age of having children in primary school, saw no good reason why they should take on an ever-increasing burden in order to finance the education of children who, in many cases, were not of their church nor even of their district. In 1969 the vestry gave a site for further building, but insisted that the PTA must carry the cost. Three years later the rector dug in his heels. The number on the roll was to be frozen at 190; all applications for admission were to go through him: and preference was to be given to children of parishioners.

Parents who did not belong to the Church of Ireland protested at once. The state, they pointed out, paid by far the largest share of the cost of the school, on the assumption that it was open to all. The new system meant that not only Catholics, but Methodists and Presbyterians, who had no alternative school of their own, would be left well down the queue. Not long afterwards the rector resigned from the parish and the ministry. He left behind him a parish bitterly torn by the conflict: on the one hand the vestry, who felt that they had barely foiled a takeover of a church school by outsiders; on the other hand the activists of the PTA, who believed that a fine experiment in multi-denominational education had been frustrated by the narrow outlook of the vestry.

From a detached position, it appears that the PTA was at war not with the parish but with the whole national school system. For the fact is that the kind of school the Dalkey parents wanted is not provided for within the educational system of the Republic: they could secure it only by taking over a parish school established within the ambiguous system inherited from the nineteenth century. The parents subsequently formed a committee to investigate the possibility of launching a community national school—multi-denominational, co-educational—owned by the parents and run by a lay committee of management. There is nothing in the departmental rules to say that such a school could not be recognised and given full state aid within the national system. It could be an interesting experiment in integrated education. There is no indication, however, that the Department of Education is interested in promoting such experiments. It is not guilty of dividing children, on religious grounds, into sheep and goats; but it recognises two colours of sheep, and two only.

Secondary Education

The national school system was created to serve the needs of the peasantry and the lower orders. The upper classes sent their children to England to school, as soon as railways and steamships made regular crossings possible. A number of select preparatory schools existed to prepare boys for English public schools: a few still survive, an odd anachronism, to the present day. But middle-class Protestants depended largely on the grammar schools in the principal towns. A haphazard growth of private academies and charitable foundations, they were far too miscellaneous to be called a system of education. In the nineteenth century there was a corresponding growth of Catholic schools, mostly run by religious orders. Protestants always felt that their institutions were socially superior, and on this ground they always attracted a few Catholics. The *Catholic Bulletin* in 1927 was able to warn its readers that this 'disease' was still 'especially virulent' in Dublin; from houses in the (high-class) Ballsbridge area 'fully a hundred Catholic children issue forth each morning to attend Protestant and godless secondary schools. . . . For such parents the pervert, the secularist, the atheist, all these have special merit as educators. . . . They think they are being exalted by being brought in contact through their children with their non-Catholic fellow-citizens.'[8]

The state was early in taking a hand in primary education. It was late in picking up any comparable responsibility for secondary education. It was not until the 1960s that the Department of Education set about imposing the doctrine of equal opportunity on a system established to provide privilege. Its method of doing so has been two-handed: one hand has dispensed grants in such a way as to provide free admission to existing schools; the other hand has been busy planning new types of school—comprehensive and community schools—which appear to be intended to replace the traditional secondary school. There are times when it appears that the right hand does not know what the left hand is doing.

* * *

Ten years ago there were still over forty Protestant secondary schools in the Republic, and more than half of these—comprising far more than half of the school places—were in Dublin. No Dublin child was out of reach of a day school; fees were moderate, and there were scholarships to ease the path of the clever child. In all, about three-quarters of the young Protestants in the city area went on to secondary schooling. For country families the difficulties were much greater. For a child from Skibbereen, say, or Westport, no Protestant school was accessible except a boarding school. Although scholarships did something to iron out the inequalities, parents in the country often made considerable sacrifices to send their children away to boarding school; and they did so, presumably, because they thought that Protestant education was worth paying for.

On the whole the boarding schools were plain institutions with little odour of public school snobbery about them. What distinguished the education of the young Protestant from that of the young Catholic was, above all, that it was in the hands of laymen. Although most of the schools have denominational affiliations, all Protestant education is essentially lay education; and this gives it a very different character from Catholic secondary education, which has been built up on the religious orders. The religious orders have in effect subsidised secondary education in Ireland for over a century; Protestant lay schools, because they represent such a small minority, have had to function within a system built up around Catholic religious schools.

The benevolent founders of the Protestant schools had in mind as a rule the twin purposes of preserving the reformed faith and redeeming the little papists from superstition and priestcraft. The King's Hospital (the Bluecoat School) in Dublin was set up by Charles II in 1670 to educate the sons of impoverished gentlefolk. Midleton College, near Cork, was endowed just before 1700 by the celebrated Betty Villiers, mistress of the same Charles, out of her immoral earnings. Royal Schools were founded in plantation areas—Cavan and Raphoe—and grammar schools in Dundalk, Drogheda and Bandon. The High School, Dublin, is the fruit of a bequest by Erasmus Smith, who was granted large estates under the Cromwellian settlement. Mountjoy and a number of affiliated schools originated in the charter schools of the Incorporated Society for the Promotion of Protestant Schools in Ireland, a proselytising body of the eighteenth century.

In most of the school boards there is a strong denominational flavour, though this is never reflected directly in the enrolment. Wesley College is run by the Methodists and St Andrew's by the Presbyterians; Newtown (Waterford) and Drogheda are associated with the Society of Friends. Most of the others have boards graced by bishops. There are a few schools which describe themselves as non-denominational; but, as an elderly relative used to say firmly, 'Any non-denominational school is a Protestant school.'

They are all, broadly speaking, independent foundations, privately owned, governed by more or less self-perpetuating boards. To mobilise a group like this for any common policy has always been rather like activating the League of Nations. In the lean years after 1922 they had job enough to survive. In 1965 a special report presented to the General Synod of the Church of Ireland had to say that the situation was critical.

> To arrest the downward drift in Protestant secondary education is not going to be easy, to reverse the trend is a truly formidable task. All concerned—the churches, the government, the governors of the schools, the teachers, and above all the parents—will have to take secondary education much more seriously in future if Irish standards are not to fall far behind those obtaining elsewhere in Europe. For Protestants there is the further risk that their educational standards will fall below those of the rest of Ireland.[9]

Change and decay was not an unfamiliar situation for the minority; but this time they did something about it. A committee was formed representing all the Protestant denominational interests to work out a common policy for secondary education. In 1973 the committee was able to report, with modest satisfaction, that the strictures of the 1965 report 'would not be deserved today'.[10]

By a process of amalgamation the number of schools had been

greatly reduced, and nearly all had gone co-educational.* The King's Hospital parted with its magnificent eighteenth-century evidence. At Cootehill, Co. Cavan, there has been substantial and moved westwards. Mountjoy left its Dickensian tenements in the north city and moved to the northern suburbs. High School, Alexandra, Wesley and St Andrew's all migrated to the southern suburbs. This building programme was helped, from 1963 onwards, by the provision of state capital for secondary school buildings. Even so, it represented an impressive investment, not only of private funds, but of time, energy and confidence.

* * *

In 1966 the Department of Education, with its right hand, laid on the table its plan for free secondary education. In order to open up access to secondary schools the government proposed to subsidise the education of every pupil in a day school by up to £25 a head per year. The majority of Catholic schools joined the scheme, and the number of children moving from primary to secondary education took an instant leap upwards. The Protestant schools, however, were more hesitant. Firstly, no Protestant school could hope to pay its way on £25 a year, because lay teachers have to be paid a living wage, while teachers in religious orders do not. Secondly, the children most underprivileged in the Protestant community were those in the country areas, and the department firmly ruled out any provision for boarding school fees. It seemed, therefore, that no Protestant child could get any benefit from the free-school scheme unless he attended a Catholic day school.

The department conceded the anomaly but could not see any way to correct it. Eventually the minister simply handed over a block grant of £300,000 to the Protestant committee and left them to dole it out.

Some teachers argue that the committee made a tactical error in accepting this solution. 'They shouldn't have taken the minister off the hook,' one of them said to me. The sum of money allocated was fair enough, but equal money is not the same thing as equal opportunity. The committee tried to apply the funds where need was greatest, by making grants-in-aid to

---

* At the time of writing the total is twenty-eight—fifteen in the Dublin area, thirteen outside—but other amalgamations are under way.

F

pupils on the basis of a means test. In 1973 the maximum grant covered nearly 60 per cent of a pupil's boarding school fees, then around £350 a year. By mid-1975 the grant covered only about 40 per cent of an annual fee which had soared to about £600.

All the same, the anomaly remained. Free education did not extend to Protestants. The department, sensitive to any charge of discrimination, decided to rectify the balance by putting in its left-hand package. Comprehensive schools—combining the grammar school and the technical school streams—had been established in three rural centres. The department now promoted and aided the transformation of two Dublin schools—Mountjoy on the north side and Avoca on the south—into free Protestant comprehensive schools. It may seem that 'Protestant comprehensive' is itself a contradiction in terms. But what is really emerging, under the code-name Protestant, is the lay school in a new and modernised form. And it is becoming clear that, in Dublin at least, the modern lay school makes an appeal to Catholics as well as Protestants.

The new Mount Temple—which has absorbed Mountjoy and a girls' high school, Bertrand and Rutland—has a roll of 250 boys and 270 girls, all day pupils. They pay no fees. The school is the property of the state, which meets all charges and has put a large sum of money into new buildings. The board of management is, in the letter of the law, appointed by the Minister for Education. In practice the minister appoints two officials to represent the public interest, and invites three nominations from the Anglican Archbishop of Dublin. The archbishop has nominated a Church of Ireland rector, a Presbyterian minister, and a professor of Trinity College. (Government departments, it should be noted in passing, have a tendency to confer representative status on bishops.)

Formally Mount Temple is non-denominational; but the schools it replaced existed to serve the Protestant community and the continuation of this service is regarded as a primary obligation. All the same, admissions have been upwards of one-third Catholic since the first year; there are between eighty and ninety Catholic pupils on a roll of 520, and the proportion may well go up to fifty per cent. All pupils take religious instruction together from a specialist lay teacher.

New Park (formerly Avoca) has shown an even more remarkable growth—from 240 in June 1972 to 565 in September 1973—and is expected to reach 800. There is a 'huge demand' for places from Catholics. Priority is given to Protestant applicants, but it is expected that Catholics will end up as one-third of the roll.

Obviously this degree of mixing means a dilution of the traditionally Protestant character of the schools. Free education, with all the resources of state funds for buildings and facilities, must be a powerful attraction. But some Catholics are enrolling also in fee-paying schools. The King's Hospital is essentially a Church of Ireland foundation—the headmaster is a clergyman, and any nominee to the board of fifty governors must be approved by the Bishop of Meath, the Archbishop of Dublin and the Archbishop of Armagh. The board decided to remain outside the comprehensive scheme because it felt that boarding schools must be kept in existence to cater for the rural Protestant. It has built handsome new buildings near Lucan, to take in 350 boarders and 150 day pupils—boys and girls in more or less equal numbers. Here—where the headmaster says frankly: 'What I value is the Protestant way of life with its emphasis on freedom of thought'—some forty or fifty young Catholics have enrolled with almost ten times as many Protestants. More will be welcome, though priority for places will always go to Protestants. Has mixing created problems? 'Absolutely none.'

* * *

The department's left-hand formula—the comprehensive school—has been accepted in Cork city and in the small town of Raphoe, Co. Donegal. In both places a kind of hostel is run privately to provide boarding facilities. Sligo, Bandon, Kilkenny and the remaining independent schools continue to exist on the right-hand formula: pupils pay fees but get relief by way of grants through the churches' secondary education committee. Parents accept the burden of fees because they value Protestant schools, or even because they value smaller schools. 'The price of free education', a headmaster said, 'may be inferior education.'

The paradox of the country areas is that the Protestants are too *weak* to accept integration. It can be faced more boldly, perhaps, in an area where the minority is strong enough to feel some self-confidence as a community, even though, for the same reasons, the traditional antagonisms may be more in evidence. At Cootehill, Co. Cavan, there has been substantial progress in integrating Protestant children into a comprehensive school. This is a border county where the minority group numbers about 15 per cent—more or less equally divided between Church of Ireland and Presbyterian. By tradition as well as topography they belong to Ulster. After partition their loyalties still extended across the border, to the North and to Britain; and until the last decade or so they lived very much their own social life within their own religious enclave. In 1966 the comprehensive school was founded, with a board of management consisting of two nominated officials and a local priest. It has built a roll of around 550, and of these 12 per cent to 15 per cent—about the same proportion as in the population of the area—are Protestants. Most of them come from small-farm families, aggressively Protestant in the Ulster Scots tradition; but they appear to settle in happily enough with the Catholic majority, and the staff are unaware of any internal segregation or 'ganging up'. Protestant boys have one distinction: no doubt because of their background in the church hall, they are always the stars at table-tennis.

Recent years have seen a subsidence at the very foundations of the traditional secondary system. Religious vocations have been declining, especially in the teaching orders, and some orders have made the decision to withdraw from the educational field altogether. The future will depend more and more on the professional lay teacher, and an increasing share of costs will have to be borne by the state. In such a situation it may be impossible for Protestants to afford, or for the state to offer them, the luxury of segregation. Understandably, there are many who view the prospect of assimilation with misgiving. 'We have thirty day boys; the Catholic school has eight hundred,' a country headmaster said. 'If thirty went into eight hundred, assimilation would not be the word to use—it would be annihilation!'

The University

Trinity College, Dublin, was founded by a charter of Queen

Elizabeth on the lands of a former monastery 'near Dublin'. In course of time Dublin grew to embrace it. Today it occupies a location that must be almost unique : an oasis of handsome buildings, quiet squares and playing fields in the heart of the capital city. The University of Dublin is a kind of incorporeal spirit which inhabits the body of Trinity College. In consequence, the government of the college has been, throughout its history, almost identical with the government of the university.

From the Restoration onwards Trinity was closely identified with the Established Church and the Protestant Ascendancy. Indeed, the Divinity School, in which most of the clergy of the Church of Ireland were trained, was almost the hub of the university. Dissenters and Catholics were admitted during the 1790s, but their presence did little to dilute the prevailing Anglican ethos. By 1900, with the tide of Catholic power rising all around, Trinity had become the principal bulwark of Protestant conservatism. A proposal to enlarge the university, so as to embrace a college for Catholics, was abandoned in the face of stubborn opposition from the governing board and the Fellows. Instead the government founded the National University of Ireland, which was non-denominational in law, but in practice Catholic. From 1908 onwards the two institutions existed side by side—one loyalist and Protestant, the other nationalist and Catholic. It took the threat of a shotgun wedding, at the hands of an impatient Minister for Education, to bring them in 1967 to the threshold of co-operation.

If Trinity can be regarded as the powerhouse of the Anglo-Irish intellectuals, it must be said that, almost without reserve, they committed their intellect and their influence to the maintenance of entrenched privilege. Behind their high walls the Trinity dons occupied a kind of academic cosmos in which the brightest planets were Oxford and Cambridge, while London remained the centre of the solar system. All this is not to say that Trinity was a rich man's college. From very early times it always had a place for poor scholars : a boy 'of limited means' could win a sizarship which provided not only free education but free rooms and dinners. Indeed, the sons of the rich and the nobility tended to go to English universities, as they went to English schools. The bulk of the Trinity students were the sons of the squireens, the clergy, the Dublin doctors

and lawyers. For many of them the university was a spring-
board which would launch them out of the unpromising environment of Ireland into the greater opportunities of Hong Kong or
Hyderabad. The institution which carried out this function contained within itself all the contradictions of Anglo-Ireland:

> Trinity College is Irish, not English; though she is not Irish
> as most of Ireland is. Perhaps the herald who devised her
> coat of arms foresaw what she was to be. He gave her two
> square towers, battlemented, strong and unadorned. On them
> are two flags, and the two flags blow different ways.[11]

In 1916 Trinity was the headquarters of the Crown forces
in central Dublin: field guns were parked in the squares and
the front gates were barricaded against the rebels. The gates
remained barricaded, in a sense, for thirty years. Students
defied the new régime by extravagant demonstrations of loyalty
to the old. The college authorities nailed their colours to
protocol: they recognised the Governor-General of the Irish
Free State, of course, but they insisted on saluting him with
'God Save the King'. Gestures like these, pathetic rather than
arrogant, were symptomatic of a real isolation from the life of
the new Ireland.

Isolation was not entirely Trinity's fault. In 1919 the Roman
Catholic hierarchy had pronounced it unlawful for a Catholic
parent to send a child to any non-Catholic school or university
without express permission. The effect was to reduce the proportion of Catholic students in Trinity from around twenty per
cent to ten per cent or less. The bishops, in effect, had sealed
the college into its cultural *cul de sac*. The question that loomed
throughout the 1930s was whether it would survive at all.
Financially the college was dependent mainly on fees (the
legendary endowments had dwindled very much and made only
a small contribution to the budget). To keep up the fee-income
it had to keep up the intake of students; and to keep up the
intake of students—when over ninety per cent of the people
were banned from passing the gates—it was necessary to keep
entrance standards low and to take a large proportion of
foreign students. By the time war came it was apparent that
the sums would not work out. Trinity had been reduced to the
classic Anglo-Irish situation of genteel poverty.

The governing board, nevertheless, made no effort to solicit help from the state; and the explanation must lie partly in the composition of the board itself. The average age of its members had fallen by the 1940s (from a memorable peak of seventy-five in 1897), but it was still over sixty. This meant that it was made up of men who had enjoyed their student careers in the palmy days of Victoria, and who had lived two-thirds of their lives under the Crown. They had no complaint against the native government, but they did not really trust it. They thought that the state would help Trinity, but at a price. The price would be the acceptance of conditions which would prejudice the independence of the university. At the very least, it was supposed that the government would require Irish to be made a compulsory subject in the entrance examinations.

When the approach was made at last, it was made under pressure from below. In 1946 a meeting of the Junior Fellows called on the board to approach the government for financial assistance. The board accepted the resolution, though not without some finger-wagging: the Junior Fellows, it implied, might live to rue the day. A deputation headed by the Provost waited on the Minister for Finance and presented a request for £35,000 to balance the books. The minister immediately agreed to make the grant, and there was no mention of 'conditions'. In college it was widely believed that the favourable response was due to a personal intervention by the Taoiseach, Mr de Valera (who happened, incidentally, to be Chancellor of the National University).

The government grant introduced a new era in relations between the university and the state and greatly strengthened the hand of the new college administration which took over in 1952. The new Provost was Dr A. J. McConnell, a brisk Ulsterman from Ballymena. He was the first post-Treaty graduate to hold that office, and as a mathematician he was *persona grata* with Mr de Valera, himself reputedly a mathematical scholar gone astray. With the confidence of state support, his administration was enabled to think in terms of development. Buildings were refurbished, a new library was built, student numbers moved upwards from 2,500 in 1952 to 3,000 in 1960 and 4,000 in 1970, and the staff-student ratio was pushed down. At the same time the state contribution moved progressively upwards to become the mainstay of the budget. In 1960–61 the total budget was something over £500,000, of which the state contributed just under 40 per cent. By 1972–73 the total ran to £3,737,481, with a state contribution of almost £3,000,000 —not far short of 80 per cent. In plainer terms, the tax-payer was contributing something over £720 for every full-time student.

Through the early years of the new relationship the college authorities kept a wary eye on academic freedom, by which they meant, essentially, the right of a private institution to spend public money. It was unreasonable to suppose that the state would continue to pump in subsidies on these terms. In 1967 Mr Donogh O'Malley, then Minister for Education, fathered a plan for the merger of Trinity College and the Dublin college of the National University into a new University of Dublin. The academic staffs of both institutions combined in opposition to the minister's plan. In 1970 they came up with an alternative plan providing for a substantial measure of co-operation. It now seems that future policy will be based on a close integration of independent institutions, under the aegis of Mr O'Malley's Higher Education Authority.

On Trinity's part this further development in the relationship with the state reflects a fundamental change in the relationship with the community. The ban on attendance of Catholic students had been maintained with especial zeal by the Archbishop of Dublin, Dr McQuaid. In the freer atmosphere of the 1960s, however, the number of Catholic students took a turn upwards, in spite of the ban. In 1970 the hierarchy suddenly changed course, and the ban on Trinity was lifted. The Catholic schools responded at once by entering pupils for Trinity's entrance and scholarship examinations, and within a very few years there was a radical change in the composition of the student body. There is no official breakdown of students by religion, but in 1973–74 Catholics may be as many as sixty per cent. The change shows up in the official statistics as a rise in entrants from the Republic, with a corresponding drop in entrants from abroad. In 1966 students from the Republic made up 354 of an entry of 848 (40 per cent). In 1970 the native entry had risen to 641 out of a total of 877 (73 per cent). Inter-denominational relations within the college are so good that most students are simply unaware of distinctions. Two Roman Catholic chaplains share the work of pastoral care with two Deans of Residence of the Church of Ireland, plus a Presbyterian and a Methodist chaplain. The college chapel has been opened to worship by all the denominations having regular chaplains, and mass is said there every morning.

Present plans call for a rise to 6,000 students with accommodation in a large new arts block along Nassau Street, and residential accommodation on the site for about 600. Overseas students are to be held to a limit of 10 per cent. This group, of course, includes students from Nigeria and many other outposts of the sometime Empire which have had a long and close connection with Trinity, and their presence adds greatly to the character of the college.

One point of some concern, in this overall development, is the decline in the number of students from Northern Ireland. One of the *raisons d'être* of Trinity was that, even after partition, it remained an all-Ireland university. Many of its most distinguished graduates came from Northern homes, and there was always a hope that their years in Dublin would persuade them that the South, after all, was not a foreign country. In 1968 they made up just a little over one-third of the total intake, with 343 out of a total of just over a thousand. By 1970 their numbers had fallen to 141 and the proportion to 16 per cent. Many factors are at work here, no doubt. All the same, the drop appears to reflect a new perspective in Northern Protestants. Trinity, they may well feel, has gone over to the other side.

13
'Protestant Preferred'

Grocery, provisions and hardware. Wanted, young man, Protestant, T.T.

Hosiery, haberdashery: experienced lady, Protestant, for above.

Boot Dept, energetic young man. State experience, religion, and salary required.   *Irish Times* (1927)

A N D what one may very well ask, had the energetic young man's religion to do with his ability to sell boots? But in 1927, when these advertisements appeared in the *Irish Times*, it was far from unusual to associate religion with employment. Jobs are—ask any Derry man—the acid test of discrimination.

Irish country people used to say that there is no such thing as a poor Protestant. It is not true, of course, and it was never true—literally. There were always some Protestants among the manual workers and the poorest class of farmers. If one can equate illiteracy with poverty, there is some indication in the fact that in Toormore (in West Cork) in 1901 there were 56 illiterates among 284 members of the Church of Ireland—just over 9 per cent. But there were 99 illiterates among 393 Catholics—over 20 per cent.

Generally speaking, Protestants had better land and more of it. The planters knew what they were doing: if one looks at Donegal, for instance, one finds that the Protestant settlement runs along the most fertile part of it, the Finn valley. When partition began to be seriously discussed, Whitehall was floored by the problem of running a boundary between Catholic and Protestant areas in Co. Tyrone, because the Catholics occupied all the high ground (the poor mountainy farms) and the Protestants all the low ground. Within the Republic the 1961 census lists over 24,000 so-called 'farmers' with less than fifteen acres of land, but only 649 are Protestants. At the other end of the scale, Protestants make up 1,057 out of 4,682 farmers with more than two hundred acres—nearly a quarter. To look at the figures from the other end, 58 per cent of all Protestant farmers had holdings of fifty acres or more, compared with 33 per cent of Catholics.

In the city the 'poor' Protestants were to be found mainly among tradesmen, in the humbler office jobs and in domestic service. The list of parents who entered children at the Church of Ireland school in Dalkey in 1891 gives an interesting cross-section of occupations:

Coastguard	Clerk
Policeman	Shoemaker
Gardener	Dairyman
Sexton	Commission agent
Watchmaker	Labourer
Railwayman	Butler
Shopkeeper	Brickworker
Auctioneer[1]	

They were respectable citizens, and they would have been very affronted, no doubt, if they had been grouped among 'the poor'. The poor were people for whom they took up collections on Sundays.

In the professions and in the upper reaches of the business world Protestants held a commanding position right up to the Great War. In 1914 they held 70 per cent of all positions in the bank service and 66 per cent of the jobs in insurance, and they accounted for 60 per cent of the practising lawyers. As late as 1926 they still counted more than one-half of the bank employees, not much less than one-half of the chartered accountants, over one-third of the auctioneers and one-third of the insurance officials. In the professions they numbered over one-third of the lawyers, one-third of the dentists and about one-fifth of the doctors. Firms like Guinness's were notorious for employing only Protestants in senior posts. (Among Protestants, incidentally, they were also notorious for their preference for graduates of Oxford or Cambridge over those of Trinity, which suggests that their bias may have been social rather than religious.)

By and large, a society which believed in private enterprise accepted the right of a private businessman to 'look after his own'. It was another matter when jobs were in the public service and salaries came from the public purse. An historian has pointed out that, because England and Ireland continued to have separate administrations after the Union, Catholic Emancipation by no means ended Protestant Ascendancy. In the Ireland of the Garrison, office was dependent on patronage, and patronage was conditional on religion. It was true, of course, that well-educated and qualified Catholics were relatively scarce; their section of the community was educationally under-privileged until well into the present century. But even allowing for disparity in educational standards, the distribution of official appointments can only be explained by blatant discrimination. Thus in 1911, of the eighteen judges of the High Court fifteen were Protestants. A similar imbalance ran through the whole official hierarchy.[2]

At local level the act of 1898, which introduced representative local government, transferred the power of patronage from the landlords to the organised nationalists. 'With the control of seats', an observer noted, 'there passes as a corollary the control of the patronage for positions such as those of clerk, workhouse-master, rate collector, dispensary doctor and the like, which were formerly retained in the hands of the Garrison.'[3] In 1902 some heat was generated by the appointment of a Protestant lady, Mrs Dickie, as Inspector of Boarded-Out Children. A resolution from Fermoy Board of Guardians neatly tangles up the two grounds of complaint:

We also wish to know the reason for appointing a Protestant in a Catholic country to inspect children almost exclusively Catholic, and we call the attention of the Local Government Board and the Irish Government to the fact that in the Superior Courts, County Courts, and Petty Sessions Courts, Protestant judges and magistrates are in an immense majority . . . that in the Chief Secretary's office 31 Protestants and only five Catholics are employed . . . and we declare this unjust and intolerant; and we demand justice and our right-ful share of all public appointments.[4]

An apologetic reply came from Lord Monteagle:

> It would, I am confident, have been an immense advantage to all concerned if the inspector had been a Roman Catholic, but I cannot agree that her being a Protestant can fairly be regarded as a disqualification.

His Lordship had picked up the right scent. There was more to the Guardians' letter than a demand that Catholics should have a fair share of public appointments. There was also an implication that for certain posts *no* Protestant could be considered the best candidate. The same theme was resumed, thirty years on, in the Mayo library case (see pages 100-1).

An acute analysis of jobbery was made in 1915 by Professor Arthur Clery. Men of all religions, he noted, mixed well in business, but 'all the friendliness is to a certain extent like the fraternisation of soldiers in opposing trenches . . . a single shot, a blast on the trumpet, a tap on the drum, and they rush to take their places in the opposing firing lines'. The fight for official appointments was a kind of unending guerrilla war; the institution of competitive examinations for any post invariably led to an increase in Catholic appointments. Protestants were very successful in trade, both wholesale and retail, much of which was in the hands of Freemasons. From the hardware and ironmongery trades, in particular, Catholics were almost entirely excluded. Professor Clery's study is particuarly interesting on Protestant solidarity:

> When the last Protestant leaves the room the subject commonly arises. Catholics complain that Protestants always 'stick together', and that while Catholics give a fair share of their business to Protestants, while Catholic convents and even Catholic bishops employ Protestant solicitors and doctors, on the other hand . . . no Protestant tongue is submitted to Catholic eyes, no Protestant brief goes astray, the Protestant purchaser looks for Protestant potatoes, Protestant mutton, Protestant patent medicines. Of course this is an exaggeration, but there is a sufficient element of truth in it. Irish Protestants are at least as cohesive in such matters as, say, Irishmen in America. They will in most cases give preference to a less competent Protestant over a more competent Catholic.

. . . I dare say when the door slams on the last Catholic the Protestants tell each other a different story.[5]

* * *

Under a native government it was obvious that the minority could not retain a preferential position. What many of them feared was that the balance would swing the other way. In fact, the Free State set a high standard of equity in the matter of public appointments. Established civil servants were given the option of transferring to the Irish service or moving to the United Kingdom, and one may assume that the real diehards moved out. Public boards were set up to deal with appointments in central and in local government, and their fairness has rarely been called in question. All the same, not many Protestants thought of making a career in the Irish civil service. No doubt some were deterred by the need to qualify in Irish; but this may have been less a real obstacle than a symbol of a service in which they expected, instinctively, to feel out of place.

Census figures show that Protestants still tend more to private business than to the public service. In 1961 there were no more than 89 among 1,970 (male) officials in senior grades in the civil service and local authorities—about 4·5 per cent. There were only 186 Protestants among the 8,500 members of the defence forces, and no more than fifty among the 6,300 sergeants and lower ranks of the police. Among 'directors, managers and company secretaries', on the other hand, they numbered almost one-third. A survey published in the *Irish Times* claims that, of senior executives in Irish business, 24 per cent are Protestants.[6] Coming down to individual businesses one can only use a process of divination. The magazine *Hibernia* published in 1972 a guide to senior personnel in Irish banks. By going through the biographies and using the customary indicators (name, with caution; schooling) one can reckon that there are about fifty Protestants among two hundred senior staff in the Bank of Ireland and Allied Irish Banks groups.*[7] The same system (admittedly fallible) applied to the bank boards suggests that there are about sixteen Protestants among the forty-four directors of the groups—roughly one-third.

---

* These are the two Southern-based groups. The tally would be higher if one counted in the Ulster and Northern Banks, both of which are based in Belfast, though they do a lot of business in the Republic.

The tradition of the 'Protestant firm' is, of course, dying fast. In recent years the pressure of modern business has produced some remarkable examples of fusion between apparently incompatible cells. Irish whiskey has become an ecumenical product with the merger of John Jameson's (Protestants, officers and gentlemen) with the Catholic firms of Power's and Cork Distilleries. The blending of boards appears to have been carried out quite smoothly : money still creates its own social order. At the other end of the scale of affluence there is no rivalry : there are only 652 Protestants among more than 48,000 labourers and unskilled workers.

* * *

In the professions the balance has tilted quite sharply. Excluding religious of all kinds, the 1961 census return shows some 56,000 men and women in 'professional and technical occupations', and of these just about one-tenth are Protestants. By long-established custom the government normally appoints one Protestant judge to the bench of the High Court, so a Protestant lawyer probably has a rather better than average chance of achieving this highly prized distinction. It can be argued that this convention is discrimination in reverse; but it can be justified as a guarantee to the minority of equal treatment before the law.

In the law one must be meticulous about equality, since there is only one set of courts for everyone. But there is another way to deal with discrimination, and that is to institutionalise. This, as we have seen, is the system that applies in education; this is the system that still survives—sustained by a combination of tradition and self-interest—in the Dublin hospitals. When the Free State came into being it found itself with a hospital system which was partly public and partly private. The public hospitals had developed from the workhouses set up under the Poor Law and served mainly the rural areas. But in Dublin—and similarly, on a smaller scale, in Cork and in Limerick—there was a network of private hospitals, controlled by voluntary and largely self-perpetuating boards of governors.

Like the private schools, the private hospitals had their origins in charity, qualified by bigotry. Dr Steevens' Hospital was opened in 1733, Mercer's in 1734. The Rotunda, said to have been the first maternity hospital in the British dominions, opened the doors of its handsome classical building in 1757. The patients were the poor, of all denominations. (Ladies of the gentler sort, of course, were brought to bed in their own residences.) But the institutions themselves were Protestant : that is to say, the benefactors who built them, the governors who ran them, the medical staffs who served in them were ordinarily members of the Established Church. The Adelaide, a nineteenth-century foundation, had entrenched clauses in its charter providing that no Catholic might hold a medical appointment. The Catholics responded to this exclusivism by setting up hospitals of their own, working mainly through the religious orders. St Vincent's was founded by the Sisters of Charity in 1834, the Mater Misericordiae by the Sisters of Mercy in 1856.

The entire medical service of the capital city reflected this curious apartheid. Medical students from Trinity did their clinical studies in Sir Patrick Dun's or the Adelaide and their midwifery in the Rotunda. Medical students from University College went to the Mater, Vincent's and Holles Street. Appointments were made by the hospital board (usually on the advice of a medical board). The boards, of course, invariably chose the best-qualified candidate : by a happy accident it turned out that the best-qualified candidate in a Catholic hospital was always a Catholic, and the best-qualified candidate in a Protestant hospital was always a Protestant. Doctors tended to work the system on its own terms—Protestant doctors sent their patients to Protestant hospitals. All round, of course, the great majority of patients—in all the hospitals—were Catholics; and it must be said that, in spite of the eccentricities of the system, I have never heard of a case in which a patient's right to the best treatment available was dependent either on his religion or on his purse.

In general the two systems, the Catholic and the Protestant, lived side by side, accepting apartheid as the normal condition of life. In 1949, however, they came to a collision, deliberately engineered by Catholic interests, with the coup at the Meath Hospital. A group of Catholics, organised by the Knights of Columbanus, gained voting rights by the simple process of paying a small subscription. At the annual general meeting they turned up in force, voted out the existing board, and put in a board of their own. The coup was contested in the High

Court but the action was thrown out by Mr Justice Gavan Duffy. A private member's bill was then passed through the Dáil and in effect restored the status quo.[8] A participant in the struggle tells me that the Roman Catholic Archbishop of Dublin, Dr J. C. McQuaid, used his influence to secure this turnabout.

The pressure that mattered, in fact, was not sectarian but financial. By the 1920s all the voluntary hospitals of both denominations were already feeling the strain, as medical practice became more specialised and more costly. The Irish Hospitals Sweepstake provided some funds for development, though the Adelaide in Dublin and the Victoria in Cork refused, on conscientious grounds, to accept aid from a lottery. But all the hospitals continued to show heavy deficits on running costs year by year. The gap could only be bridged by public funds, which inevitably carried some measure of public control. Rationalisation, though seen to be inevitable, has been handled with caution. The Protestant voluntary hospitals formed a federation some years ago and rationalised their services; in due course a new teaching hospital, St James's, will absorb at least three of them. A public hospitals board will take over the appointment of medical staff. Meanwhile there is closer collaboration than ever before between the two wings of Dublin medicine.

* * *

The system of dual institutions—school, university, hospital—enabled some Protestants to live in a kind of mental reservation, secure from any real contact with Catholics. In some respects it suited both sides. In medicine, for instance, it was understood to reflect a deep-seated difference in philosophy and professional ethics between Catholic and Protestant doctors. Dualism was nurtured, therefore, in other spheres of life. The Boy Scouts, for instance, though non-denominational in theory, had inescapable associations with the British Raj, and hence they were unacceptable to Catholic-nationalist Ireland; so a rival organisation, the Catholic Boy Scouts of Ireland, was founded. The late Archbishop of Dublin, Dr J. C. McQuaid, used his authority very firmly in the 1940s to break up the collaboration of Catholics and Protestants in social and charitable work. Sports clubs tended to prolong the segregation of schooling: a

Protestant boy from the High School would go on to play rugby
for Wanderers.

To a great extent this kind of segregation was part of the
social convention of the day, accepted heedlessly by nine out
of ten people on both sides of the frontier; it did not necessarily
reflect any fundamental sectarian antagonism. The fences were
already going down before the *aggiornamento* of the 1960s, and
today they survive rather like an ancient embankment, long
since overgrown and discernible only in a bird's-eye view.
Although separate charitable organisations exist, they work
together freely; Protestants and Catholics co-operate in services
like 'meals on wheels' for the old; in the boy scout movement
there is close collaboration and even some talk of a merger.

In this changed situation, what becomes of the organisations
whose prime function was to protect the entrenched positions?
The Knights of Columbanus have already been noticed in the
Meath Hospital case. Their much older counterparts on the
Protestant side are the Freemasons.

The Masons—or, to give them their proper title, the Free
and Accepted Masons of Ireland—have for years been the bogey
under Ireland's Catholic bed. Certain priests and periodicals
ran a shrill campaign against them in the 1920s and the 1930s :
they were presented as godless atheists, as crypto-revolutionaries,
above all as truckers in every kind of jobbery. It was this gut-
reaction to Masonic influences that induced Mr Frank Aiken,
in the famous Mayo library case, to charge that 'Before one can
get a job as a candidate from the Local Appointments Commissioners, one has to be the Brother of Deputy Thrift, the
Grand Sword-Bearer.'[9] Many Protestants were far from happy
about the part the Masons appeared to play in, for example,
hospital appointments. The sometime Primate, Dr Gregg,
'steadfastly refused to join either the Freemasons or the Orange
Order. He considered a member of either organisation forfeited
independence of judgment.'[10]

A certain aura of suspicion hangs about the Order of Freemasons, principally because it remains a secret society. It is
in reality rather less secret than people imagine. Its annual
reports and accounts are available in the National Library, and
so is the little book of its laws and constitutions. The reports
contain a full list of the Grand Officers and of the Provincial

Grand Masters, as well as a list of all the lodges with their contributions to central funds during the year.

The Irish Constitution of the Order not only ranges north and south of the border, but embraces lodges in Johannesburg, Colombo, Bombay, Nairobi and a variety of other outposts of what was once the Empire. Two of the latest warrants have been issued in Ghana. In all there are over 800 lodges, with a total membership of some 60,000. In Ireland itself the great majority of lodges are in the north, but there are no fewer than seventy-five in Dublin, nine or ten in Cork, and many others scattered about the country. Taking a membership of thirty or forty to each lodge, there must be up to 3,000 members in Dublin and perhaps another thousand or so through the rest of the Republic. Their headquarters is a handsome building in Molesworth Street, Dublin.

Historically the Masons were rather egalitarian in their outlook. The bulk of Dublin members came from the lower middle class; in the country a lodge was often formed by the landlord in the Big House, with the upper servants and the local Protestant farmers as members. Part of the attraction was (and perhaps still is) the opportunity to mix with men in a higher station, in an environment in which precedence depended solely on standing within the Order. Daniel O'Connell, who had been a member before the church forbade Catholics to join, thought the Order had 'no evil tendency', except that it encouraged hard drinking; but he found 'the wanton and multiplied taking of oaths . . . alone abundantly sufficient to prevent any serious Christian from belonging to that body'.[11]

Today's membership includes a good many clergymen (including, among the Grand Officers, the Archbishop of Dublin) who must be assumed to be serious Christians. The laws state that 'The Bible, which is referred to by Freemasons as the Volume of the Sacred Law, is always open in the Lodges.' But the Order is not specifically Christian: members are required only to declare their belief in a supreme being—a formula which conveniently embraces the Jew and the Moslem as well as the Christian. Nor does it have a political philosophy, beyond a declaration that a Freemason is 'strictly forbidden to countenance any act which may have a tendency to subvert peace and the good order of society'. Southern members like to make it clear that the Masons have no connection with the Orange Order.*

Why do people join? Because they want to be initiated into the mysteries of the Order? Because they want to engage in mummery with skulls and swords and bandaged eyes? Members, says a Grand Officer, 'have a common interest in brotherhood, charity, and yes, a certain conviviality. The secrets are a minor element in Freemasonry nowadays and they nearly all relate to recognition of one member by another.' The charity is real enough. The Order runs a boarding school in Dublin for children of members who have died leaving young families or who have fallen on hard times, and it may pay the cost of higher education too. All the money is contributed voluntarily by members. For a young father, therefore, membership of the Masons represents a kind of insurance for the future of his family.

Do people join because they expect benefits in their business or profession? 'If they do, they must be disappointed,' says the same officer. 'Members are certainly not encouraged to join for this reason.' But he acknowledges that 'If you know a man through Freemasonry, you may have a tendency to lean towards him.'

The hysteria that marked attacks on the Freemasons a generation or so ago has now wholly disappeared. The Masons have established good relations with their traditional rivals, the Knights of Columbanus; representatives have visited one another's lodges and dined together. This cosy association does not entirely meet the need which some of the younger men feel for a real *raison d'être*. They would like to abandon, finally, their role as Praetorian Guard for the Protestant community; they feel that the minority now needs purpose more than it need protection. Some would like to see the Masons going into social service, not on an exclusive basis but for the whole community. They recognise that they would encounter difficulty at two levels: the conservatism of older members who dwell in the upper reaches of the Masonic cosmos, and the lingering suspicion in the minds of the plain people.

*   *   *

* The Orange Order has figured little in this book because its main activity has always been in the North. An up-to-date account can be found in Tony Gray, *The Orange Order*, London 1972.

Discrimination is a state of mind, of course. One clergyman wrote, in answer to an inquiry: 'I don't go round *looking* for discrimination.' But another was anxious to demolish 'this myth that there is no discrimination'. He had been rector of a parish in the midlands where, he said, there was an organised conspiracy to prevent any Protestant from buying land, a shop or any other property. Auctioneers would find a reason to withdraw a property from sale if a Protestant turned out to be the highest bidder. To beat the system, he had to bring in unknowns from outside the area, to bid on behalf of Protestant purchasers. That was thirty years ago. Inquiries today, in the same area, provide no evidence that the same practice continues. One must make some reservation in regard to land: the taboo on alienating land from the tribe is still a powerful force, but it operates just as much among Catholics as among Protestants.

Some appear to believe that justice can only be demonstrated by some kind of proportional representation. In 1944 a clergyman wrote that 'When twenty-two appointments were made at a new county home in Monaghan, not a single one was given to a Protestant, though the modest request for two was made.'[12] But why two? Why not twenty-two, if there were twenty-two qualified Protestant candidates—or none, if there was none? In the last analysis, too precise a balancing of equality is discrimination in itself.

14

Root and Branch

The Church of Ireland

> We have sprung up from roots of our own—we are not an
> offshoot of the English Church; we are not, as some would
> represent us, 'the English Church in Ireland'. We form a
> Church complete in herself—an ancient national Church,
> which was in existence before those Anglo-Saxon times from
> which the great Anglican Communion, with all its depen-
> dencies, derives its name. Let us, then, have the courage and
> wisdom to stand alone; let us cease from clutching at the
> apron-strings of the Anglican connection; and let the word
> Anglicanism, as describing our faith and practice, be banished
> from our vocabulary.[1]
>
> Archbishop WILLIAM CONYNGHAM PLUNKET (1869)

T H E mainstream of Protestant religious culture in Ireland is
represented by the Church of Ireland; and the Church of
Ireland, is, as Archbishop Plunket stated it, an Irish church.
Within the Republic the membership of the Church of Ireland
outnumbers the Presbyterians by six to one, and the Methodists
by more than eighteen to one. Even more evident than the
preponderance of numbers is the physical presence of the
Church of Ireland—in cathedrals, churches, graveyards.

The trappings are, perhaps, somewhat out of proportion to
its shrunken stature. In grandeur of title the bishops of the
Church of Ireland defer to no ecclesiastical dignitary anywhere:
Ossory, Ferns and Leighlin; Tuam, Killala and Achonry;
Killaloe, Kilfenora, Clonfert and Kilmacduagh. Today some of
the sees are not even spots on an ordinary road-map. Achonry,
Leighlin, Kilmacduagh are relics preserved in ecclesiastical

amber. Of the thirty-one cathedrals many are only the site of
a modest parish church. Nevertheless, these links with the pre-
Reformation church are of great importance in the thought of
the Church of Ireland. It sees itself not as a new church devised
by Martin Luther or Henry VIII, but as the ancient Catholic
Church preserving, as the core of its belief, 'the Anglican restoration of the primitive Christian faith by Protestant reform'. In
this sense it derives its legitimacy from the early Celtic Church,
the church of St Columba and St Columbanus. Right through
its most anglicised period it retained its dedications to Irish
saints: St Flannan at Killaloe and St Fachtna at Ross; St
Canice at Kilkenny and St Fethlimidh at Kilmore; St Macartan
at Clogher and St Carthage at Lismore. One of the finest sec-
tions of the Church Hymnal is the 'Hymns from Ancient Irish
Sources', beginning with that breathtaking steeplechase for
church choirs, 'The Breastplate of St Patrick'. And, though by
far the larger part of the membership for the past fifty years has
been in the North, the Church of Ireland keeps its central
organisation in Dublin, its General Synod meets at Christ
Church, and St Patrick's remains its national cathedral.

* * *

There are about four hundred parishes in all Ireland. They
are grouped into fourteeen dioceses,* and the dioceses in turn
fall into two provinces, Armagh and Dublin. Armagh is, by
long tradition, the senior province, and the Archbishop of
Armagh takes precedence over the Archbishop of Dublin. Both
bear the title of Primate, with a fine distinction: His Grace of
Dublin is Primate of Ireland; His Grace of Armagh is Primate
of *All* Ireland.

The boundaries of the dioceses were laid down in the main
in the twelfth century, and they do not conform to modern
political convenience. Certain bishops have sees that straddle
the border: Derry is united with Raphoe, which embraces the
county of Donegal, and Clogher runs from Monaghan through
into Fermanagh. Some of the dioceses of the South are very
sparsely populated, while in the West the Bishop of Tuam is
overseer of a huge area roughly equivalent to the province of
Connacht, with a church population of only about six thousand
souls.

* Some of these are united dioceses, e.g. Limerick, Ardfert and Aghadoe.

The political division has of course entailed a delicate balancing act at the level of the General Synod. Education committees, for instance, have to deal with two different educational systems and two different government departments. The prayer-book invokes a blessing 'for all in authority, and especially for (*NI* Elizabeth our Queen) (*RI* our President)'. During recent years the balancing act has become even more difficult, and there are some who argue that it has been sustained too delicately: that church leaders have not done enough to combat bigotry, to demand justice for the Northern minority, and to discountenance the concept of Protestantism as a political creed. The Bishop of Clogher, Dr Richard Hanson, told an ecumenical meeting in 1972 that all denominations in the North had become 'captive churches':

> All Christian bodies, Catholic and Protestant alike, have long ago sold their independence and their integrity to political ideologies, in return for the massive support of their people.[2]

He called on the churches to give a lead by keeping all political symbols—'Orange flags, black berets, Union Jacks, tricolours and all national anthems'—out of the place of worship. The reaction of his flock was bitter and hostile, and not long afterwards Dr Hanson resigned his see and returned to teaching theology in England. His colleagues by and large admired his integrity, but they did think that he had imperilled the unity of the church by indulging his desire to speak out. In terms of church diplomacy they can never afford to overlook the fact that the vast majority of church members in the North—and this would mean a substantial majority in the whole of Ireland —are devoted upholders of the Unionist cause.

* * *

The Irish Church Act, noted J. P. Mahaffy, 'tended inevitably to abolish the only resident gentry in the wilder parts of Ireland'.[3] The country parson would smile today—a little ruefully, perhaps—at this description of his role. He has a stipend which rarely places him above the average income of his parishioners. He has an allowance for a car, which is essential for carrying out his duties. He has a glebe house rent-free, not infrequently an old and comfortless place, far too large for an era of high fuel costs and no servants. The stipend for each parish is fixed annually by the synod of the diocese; it may not be below the minimum figure set by the General Synod (£2,000 in 1976) but it is rarely very much higher. Out of this the rector will have to make provision for a home when he retires, since the rectory belongs to the parish and will pass to his successor.

In return he makes his time (and his wife's) available to the parishioners on a seven-day week; he acts as school manager, he gives classes in religious knowledge, he attends all parish functions, he sits on all committees, he pays house-visits and he visits the sick in hospital—and, of course, he conducts services each Sunday in one or more churches.

To the layman it hardly looks like a real job: cups of tea all the week and a sermon on Sunday. In fact a good deal depends on the calibre of the man. An idler will get the chance to be idle; a recluse will be able to withdraw. It is not the kind of career to attract, in these days, many front-rank intellectuals. For the energetic man the reward comes in service—to his own little church community first of all, but, increasingly, to the larger community of which it is a part.

In the ordering of worship in a parish the rector is the sole authority, subject, of course, to his bishop (an old rule enjoins the churchwardens to inform on him if he preaches heresy). But in parish administration he is only the chairman of a committee. The select vestry, elected annually from all the parishioners— women as well as men—is responsible for raising and handling all parish funds, for keeping the church in good order and suitably prepared for divine service, and for paying at least the minimum stipend to the minister.

The affairs of the diocese are managed by the diocesan synod, consisting of all the clergy of the diocese with twice their number of elected lay members; the bishop presides. From each of the diocesan synods representatives are elected to the General Synod, the supreme assembly of the church, which sits in Dublin once a year. Apart from the bishops the synod consists of 648 members: 216 clergymen and twice as many laymen.

The laity also have a hand in church appointments. If a parish falls vacant, two representatives of the vacant parish sit on the diocesan board that will choose the new incumbent. If a diocese falls vacant, the new bishop is elected by a system of electoral colleges in which the laity hold roughly half the votes. Only the Archbishop of Armagh is chosen by the bishops themselves from among their own number.

At every level, therefore, the government of the church is subject to the democratic consent of its lay members. In this essential respect the authority of a Protestant bishop is quite different—or appears to a Protestant to be quite different—from that of a Roman Catholic bishop, who speaks always with the voice of a monolithic and strictly hierarchical church.

* * *

The hub of church organisation is the modern building at Rathmines, Dublin, which houses the Representative Church Body. The RCB was set up at the time of disestablishment to act as trustee for all the church's property. It consists of the bishop, one elected clergyman and two elected laymen from each diocese, with fourteen co-opted members. From its accounts, presented annually to the General Synod, one can form a true picture of its legendary wealth. It holds in all about £16 million in investments,* and the greater part of this is in trusts directed to a specific object—the upkeep of the church, its services and its clergy. The RCB has no legal authority to divert these funds to any other purpose. In 1973 the income available for disposal by the General Synod amounted to around £550,000. Voluntary giving remains by far the largest source of the church's revenues. Foreign missions—which might be considered out of fashion—still attract remarkable support: in 1973 a total of nearly £300,000 was subscribed to the missions through fifteen different societies.

The central problem of administration becomes more acute year by year: too many churches, too few people. A report presented by the RCB to the General Synod of 1974 called for drastic changes in the organisation of the church, so that all resources might be concentrated on the provision of clergy. 'Better', said the proposer, 'a clergyman without a building than a building without a clergyman.' But finding the men to maintain the service of the church may not be easy. Only four ordinations, the report noted, were expected in 1974.[4]

* * *

* 1973 valuation: the figure might be written down by 40 per cent in 1975 slump conditions.

The tradition of the Church of Ireland has always had within it two strands, the puritan and the Catholic. Soon after disestablishment the strength of the puritans was shown when a committee under a lay chairman—supported by some of the clergy but opposed by most of the bishops—carried out a revision of the Book of Common Prayer, designed to expunge all traces of High Church (or popish) observances. Twice—in 1923–28 and in 1934–39—parish clergy have been hauled before the court of the General Synod, at the petition of outraged parishioners, to answer for breaches of the canons.[5] In recent times the climate has become milder, and in 1964 the most contentious of the canons—Canon 36, which forbade the placing of a cross on the communion table—was repealed.

To both the Roman Catholic and the Presbyterian the position of the Church of Ireland sometimes appears equivocal. To its own champions, its character derives precisely from its blending of the two traditions. 'We believe', says the Bishop of Ossory, 'that ours is the best interpretation of the Christian faith; we have the Catholic inheritance, but the liberal method.'[6]

The Presbyterian Church

Presbyterianism was, and still remains, almost exclusively the religion of Ulster. The Presbyterian Church in Ireland claims about 400,000 members, and of these 96 per cent live north of the border. Of the 16,000 in the Republic nine or ten thousand are in the three Ulster counties—Cavan, Monaghan and Donegal.* The presbytery of Dublin and Munster, which, roughly speaking, includes all congregations south of a line drawn from Drogheda to Sligo, claims only 5,461 members—only a few hundred more than Strabane, the smallest of the Northern presbyteries; and these are spread over forty-eight congregations, giving them an average strength of around 114 members each. For comparison, the Foyle presbytery, which takes in a largely rural area east of Derry, averages about five hundred members to each congregation, and in North Belfast the average runs up to two thousand.

These demographic lines were laid out by history; what is

---

* The figure of 16,000 is taken from the 1971 census. It may not tally exactly with figures from church sources because presbyteries do not follow the political boundary.

surprising is that they have changed so little. Presbyterianism was planted in Ireland with the Scots settlers, and it has penetrated outwards very little from the orginal areas of plantation. As many as one-half of all the Presbyterians in Ireland live within a fifteen-mile radius of the centre of Belfast. South of the border, it is only in Donegal, Monaghan and Cavan that Presbyterians have both the numbers and the topographical unity that are necessary to give a real sense of community. In Dublin, the main centre outside Ulster, they are scattered throughout the fringes of the city and its suburbs; the old city-centre churches are like rocks in the ocean, to which the birds return to settle briefly every Sunday.

Irish Presbyterians share their faith with some fifty million other Christians of the reformed churches throughout the world. But Calvin's church came to Ireland by way of Scotland, and the print of Scotland is very clear in its thinking, in its loyalties, even in its forms of speech: a congregation is governed by a 'kirk-session'; a minister's house is 'The Manse'.

Presbyterianism takes its origins and its name from its rejection of episcopal government in favour of government by elected elders (*presbuteros*). The governing body of a congregation, the kirk-session, consists of the minister and the church elders. Congregations are grouped into presbyteries (twenty-two in all Ireland) and presbyteries are grouped into five regional synods. In each of these church courts, as they are called, ministers and elders sit in equal numbers. At the summit of the structure is the General Assembly, which consists of all the ministers of the church and an elder representing each of its congregations—about 1,300 delegates in all. The Moderator, who presides, is a minister, elected for one year. All ministers are equally eligible for election, since the parity of the clergy is a fundamental principle of the church. When a pastorate falls vacant the new minister receives a 'call' from the congregation. He must be approved by the whole church; and this usually involves the rather formidable ordeal of preaching a trial sermon before the assembled congregation.

Preaching the Word is a central part of the function of a minister. The church as a whole lays its stress rather on the scriptures than on the sacraments: in fact holy communion—the Lord's Supper—is celebrated in most churches from two to

six times a year only. The minister generally improvises the
prayers, though there is an authorised prayer-book on which he
may draw. The people normally sit, not kneel, during prayers.
The psalms, especially in the metrical versions, are the characteristic form of singing ('The Lord's My Shepherd' has by now
become an ecumenical property). Approval for a church hymnal
was not given until late in the last century; and even then the
old guard fought a stern rearguard action against an instru-
mental accompaniment, seeing the harmonium as the herald
of Rome.

As theologians the Presbyterian divines are much respected
by their opposite numbers of Rome : dogma, as one might say,
does not eat dogma. Their faith is founded on John Calvin's
interpretation of scriptural authority, and its supreme standard
is the Bible itself.

> The whole counsel of God concerning all things necessary for
> His own glory, man's salvation, faith and life, is either
> expressly set down in Scripture, or by good and necessary
> consequence may be deduced from Scripture; unto which
> nothing at any time is to be added, whether by new revela-
> tions of Spirit or by traditions of man.[7]

The words are those of the Westminster Confession of Faith, the
'subordinate standard' of the church. Since 1836 all ministers
and elders have been required to subscribe to the Confession,
recognising it to be 'founded on, and agreeable to, the Word of
God'. Subscription is held to bind them only to its fundamental
doctrines : they do not have to swallow literally its seventeenth-
century forms :

> There is no other head of the Church but the Lord Jesus
> Christ. Nor can the Pope of Rome in any sense be head
> thereof; but is that Antichrist, that man of sin, and son of
> perdition, that exalteth himself, in the Church, against Christ
> and all that is called God.

To a layman the doctrine of Calvin is associated inescapably
with predestination : the belief that God has divided mankind
into the righteous and the unrighteous, the saved and the
damned. This summary perhaps misrepresents the subtlety of
Calvin's thought; but it was some such version as this that

filtered through Scotland to Ireland with the early settlers, to be hardened still further when it came up against the Romanism of the Counter-Reformation. It is hard to resist the belief that this dogma of a divine élite has contributed to the rigidity of Presbyterian attitudes in social and political relationships.

With their rigid theology the early Presbyterians brought in a system of religious observance which compares in many ways with that of orthodox Jewry. Men must not work, children must not laugh and play on the Lord's Day. A traveller of the 1880s, returning to Donegal after a long absence, saw them unchanged:

> Our meeting house, too—an unattractive whitewashed building, half filled with honest, hard-looking people, all dressed in Sunday clothes, still adhering to the old habit of learning by heart the Psalms of David, Proverbs of Solomon, Prophecies of Isaiah, and the Sermon on the Mount.[8]

The Old Testament was as sacred to them as the New, and their vision of the Almighty was of Jehovah seated amidst his thunderbolts.

* * *

Presbyterians never formed part of the Ascendancy, and where they have been strong enough to form a recognisable community they appear in general to have lived on good terms with their Catholic neighbours. At a small town in Donegal, not thirty miles from the battle-scarred streets of Derry, I was told that relations 'could not be better'. In this area Presbyterians have been settled since 1620 or thereabouts, many of their farms having descended from father to son until the present time. Outside Ulster they are associated mainly with trade and commerce; their image is that of the solid citizen, industrious and well-to-do, strict but honourable. It is oddly appropriate that one of the most prominent of their churches in central Dublin is known by the name of a family of tea-merchants, as Findlater's Church.

Some of their ministers have taken an active part in the ecumenical movement, and they are highly regarded—both for their personal qualities and for their professional training—by clergy of other churches. The congregations do not disapprove, but the older people, at least, have their reservations. The

Catholic Church has always been the enemy : the Indians may be friendly today, but who knows about tomorrow?

The Methodist Church

The Methodist Church has its origins in that eighteenth-century religious revival which contemporaries, with evident distaste, described as 'enthusiasm'. The first group of Methodists met in London in 1740 : they were then, and remained almost to their founder's death, an evangelical group *within* the Church of England. Within five or six years the first of their preachers had arrived in Ireland, and John Wesley himself braved the sea-crossing for the first time in 1747. In the course of his intensely active career Wesley paid no fewer than twenty-one visits to Ireland, amounting in all to over six years of his life. He carried his message all over the island, covering incredible distances on horseback, preaching two, three and four times a day to anyone who had ears to hear.

Wesley was indignant at the indolence of the Established Church in a field in which there was such a harvest of souls to be reaped. Religious observance seems to have been at a low ebb at this period, among both Catholics and Protestants, and Wesley's fervent sincerity made a deep impression on his hearers. Again and again he notes that his audiences were 'quiet' and 'serious' : 'So civil a people as the Irish in general, I never saw, either in Europe or America.' At Ennis 'more than nine in ten of the congregation were Papists; but none spoke an unkind or uncivil word, either while I preached or when I had done'. At Tyrrellspass 'many of the neighbouring gentlemen were present, but none mocked. That is not the custom here; all attend to what is spoken in the name of God; they do not understand the making sport with sacred things; so that, whether they approve or no, they behave with seriousness.'

Some of his most attentive listeners appear to have been found among the soldiers. Probably many came of puritan backgrounds, whether in England or in Scotland, and the Anglican Church fell far short of their concept of godly living. The mission was particularly successful among the Palatine Germans, and many of these families remain staunch Methodists down to our own day.

Methodists today number about 80,000 in all Ireland. South

of the border their congregations—still shrinking—total only about 5,000. Their central body, the Methodist Conference, consists of 150 ministers and 150 laymen, and meets in alternate years in North and South. The church has invested assets of about one million pounds—managed from Dublin—but the great bulk of its income comes from voluntary giving. In the ministry of the church the tradition of the itinerant preacher is still maintained. A minister is appointed to a 'circuit' by the Conference, and he remains in the same place for no more than eight years. The system must be hard on ministers and their families; but it may not be fanciful to attribute to it, in some degree, that independent spirit which is characteristic of Methodists in all walks of life. Under this system the congregation cannot be built around the minister; the people of the church must rely on themselves to create a community.

* * *

The belief of Methodists is embracing rather than exclusive. Other denominations see it as theologically vague. Methodists would say that it embodies the whole accepted body of reformed Christian doctrine, with a special emphasis on personal religion, personal commitment, personal salvation. It sees the Christian, in Wesley's words, 'pressing on to sainthood'. The form of worship is within the discretion of the individual minister. But the most characteristic expression of their worship lies in their hymns. The Wesley brothers valued congregational singing as a communal expression of devotion and joy, and they gave a great number of the finest hymns to the stock that is common to all Protestants: hymns that range from the deep fervour of 'Jesu, Lover of my Soul' to the jubilation of 'Christ the Lord is Risen Today'.

In a remarkable way, indeed, the personality of Wesley seems to pervade the whole community of Methodists. The tradition of service, handed down from him, has inspired this small group of men and women to make an impressive contribution to the society in which they live. To look south of the border only, the Dublin Central Mission, now ninety years old, was founded to provide practical help as well as gospel teaching to the poor of the city. A residential colony for forty-five old men and women was set up a few years ago, and there are plans to put £250,000 into a social aid centre which would offer aid and shelter to the misfits of society. In the field of education, Wesley College is still the largest privately managed Protestant secondary school in the Republic, and in 1947 Methodists founded the Gorteen Agricultural College in Tipperary. In all these activities they provide the initiative, the management and the money, while other denominations get most of the benefit.

Methodists have been constantly active in the movement for greater understanding between the Christian churches. In Dublin within recent years they have provided an earnest of their belief. When the Centenary Church at St Stephen's Green—the cathedral, so to speak, of Methodism in Dublin—was gutted by fire, they decided not to rebuild. Instead they share the large parish church of the Church of Ireland at Leeson Park: services are help separately on Sunday mornings, but on Sunday evenings both denominations worship together. The funds which they might have used for rebuilding are to be applied instead to a community centre for both congregations. This decision involved swallowing a lot of institutional pride, and it cannot have been easy to reach. But the fact that it was reached at all indicates that the Methodists remain true to their tradition of serving people rather than institutions.

Friends and Brethren

After the three main Protestant churches, none of the other Christian sects in the Republic of Ireland has a membership that goes beyond three figures.* Two of the smaller groups perhaps merit a special word.

The Quakers are more properly termed the Society of Friends. Their worship is, in the words of a member, 'based on a quiet waiting for God, so that his spirit may be revealed in the heart of each person'.[9] They have dispensed with the sacraments and they have no regular clergy. Their reputation for works of charity, still strong in Ireland, must date back at least to the 1798 rebellion, when they intervened to prevent the slaughter of innocents on both sides. But their special place in the regard of the Irish was won by their works of mercy during the Famine. They were the first to recognise that what starving people needed was food; they accordingly set up soup kitchens where relief was

---

* The 1961 census records about 3,000 Jews in the Republic.

G

given to all the needy, regardless of religion. Many of their members worked unstintingly, sometimes at the risk of their lives, to aid the victims of starvation and fever.

Their religion enjoins on them the strictest honesty in business dealings, and in material terms it has served them well: they are in general comfortably off, with large interests in such industries as milling. But they have maintained their record of effort on behalf of the underprivileged; certain of their members are among the most devoted workers for itinerants, the untouchables of modern Irish society.

Their main membership—under six hundred—is in Dublin; there are almost a hundred members in Waterford and a handful each in Wexford, Limerick and Cork. A good many people, attracted by their reputation, apply to join the Society; but they are carefully examined to ensure that they are not merely drawn by some kind of sentimental appeal. Quakers are pacifists; but pacifism alone does not make a Quaker.

* * *

The Plymouth Brethren, despite their name, had their origin in Ireland. They were a product of the evangelical revival, between 1825 and 1830. Their founder, John Nelson Darby, was ordained in the Church of England after studying at Trinity College, Dublin; but he and his associates withdrew from the churches to form their own brotherhood of Christians.

The Brethren base their belief on the authority of the scriptures. They believe that justification of sinners is by faith alone, but that those who have been justified will show evidence of their rebirth by good works and holiness. There is no formal liturgy and no regular clergy; any member may conduct a service or officiate at a baptism or communion. Their total membership in Ireland runs to 20,000, but of this only a tiny fraction—about 500—is in the Republic. Although they are ardent evangelicals, they do not seek for converts: 'The Brethren remain convinced', writes one of them, 'that church membership is not the all-important question, but rather a personal relationship with God through trusting Jesus Christ as Saviour and Lord.'

15

A Member of the Nation

And oh! it were a gallant deed
To show before mankind
How every race and every creed
Might be by love combined—
Might be combined, yet not forget
The fountains whence they rose,
As, filled by many a rivulet,
The mighty Sionann flows.

THOMAS DAVIS (1843)

I T may have dawned upon the attentive reader, by this stage, that a book which purports to portray the Irish Protestant has made only passing reference to many of the most celebrated Protestant names in Irish history: Wolfe Tone and Robert Emmet, who sought to overturn British rule by force of arms; Thomas Davis, who kindled the flame of nationalism again; Isaac Butt and Charles Stewart Parnell, who carried on the fight with the weapons of parliamentary democracy. But my purpose has been to delineate the tribe, to seek out its origins, to study its pattern of behaviour; and these men are famous precisely because they broke the pattern, because they stepped out of the tribe in order to identify themselves with the Irish nation. They stand out as individuals; they did little or nothing to solve the problem of identity which confronted the tribe as a whole: did it belong to the Irish nation or did it not?

The pure doctrine of Irish nationalism descends to us from Thomas Davis, a Protestant of Anglo-Irish origins and a graduate of Trinity College. In 1842 Davis joined with a Catholic, Charles Gavan Duffy, to launch a newspaper which declared itself in its title: *The Nation*. Within three years he

was dead. But in those years he had created and left behind him
a concept of Irish nationality more comprehensive even than
that of Tone. His vision went beyond a union of men of all
creeds. It recognised the diversity of the Irish people, and it
recognised that all the diverse strains must be embraced within
a nation:

> The Milesian, the Dane, the Norman, the Welshman, the
> Scotchman and the Saxon, naturalised here, must combine,
> regardless of their blood. . . . This is as much needed as the
> mixture of Protestant and Catholic.[1]

To a modern eye the articles in *The Nation* read like sermons,
but they were sermons addressed to all the people. 'Protestant
operatives' were constantly urged to see that their interests lay
with the mass of the people, and were assured that their freedom
of religion must be respected: 'Every man, whether Presbyterian, Catholic or Protestant, should act by his own conscience
and be judged by it, and by no other man's.' Neither blood,
nor creed, nor clan—in the words of one of Davis's poems—
should bar a man from membership of the Irish nation.

* * *

The idea of nationality, in this sense, was a creation of the
nineteenth century. Under pressure of the democratic spirit that
was liberated by the French Revolution, groups of people
acquired a kind of self-consciousness which they called nationality. For Ireland, this process of self-identification came at a
peculiarly difficult period: the country was divided in politics.
in religion, and in language. And these divisions were due mainly
to the influence of a domineering neighbour which offered—
and which had tried, by the Act of Union, to force upon
Ireland—an alternative nationality. Austrians have never been
quite sure that they are not Germans; Belgians have never
been quite sure that they are not Dutch or French. The Irish
have had to reassure themselves constantly that they are not
English. 'There is no living Irishman', said Daniel Corkery,
'who is Irish through and through, as the first Englishman we
may light upon is English.'[2] To embrace all Irishmen, after
Davis's philosophy, has always been perilously close to embracing the enemy; for where do Irishmen stop and Englishmen
begin? So those who wanted to define Irish nationality have

been driven to define it by exclusion. Membership of the Irish nation has been granted upon conditions: religious conditions, political conditions, cultural conditions.

The religious condition, as we have seen, loomed up again and again in the 1920s and 1930s. Today it is out of fashion: few people are likely to suggest that you must be a Catholic in order to be an Irishman. Nevertheless, the Catholic finds that the presumptions are in his favour. He acquires membership of the nation by being born into the majority, and he can suit himself about the other conditions. The Protestant is in a somewhat different case; and even the best-intentioned effort to include him can have the effect of underlining the conditions of membership. Thus *The Bell*—which was a tireless champion of liberal values during the dismal 1940s—declared itself against discrimination:

> The names of Parnell, Smith O'Brien, Butt, Thomas Davis, Lord Edward, Tone, Emmet, Yeats, O'Casey, Hyde and many others—all Protestants—prove that when a man's political attitudes were sound his religion has never been anybody's concern.[3]

But what about a man whose political attitudes are not 'sound'? The list would be much more convincing if it left any room for the proposition that a man might be a Protestant, and a Unionist, and a patriot.

* * *

One effect of the search for identity in the last century was an upsurge of interest in the antiquarian study of the Irish heritage. The Gaelic Society of Dublin was founded in 1806, the Iberno-Celtic Society in 1818, and the Irish Archaeological Society in 1840; the Kilkenny Archaeological Society, founded in 1849, developed into the Royal Society of Antiquaries of Ireland. A glance over the early copies of its transactions shows that it was under the patronage of the nobility and gentry, and the Dean of Ossory was its president. It was the age of the gentleman amateur; Protestant gentry and clerics were active in the societies and were among the distinguished dabblers (Sir William Wilde, Oscar's father, was one of them) who laid the foundation for the specialised study of Irish antiquities. The walls of the Royal Irish Academy are hung with portraits of

the Doctors of Divinity who graced its Committee for Polite
Literature and Antiquities.

The Irish language was included among the antiquities:
although it was still, in the earlier part of the century, the
spoken tongue of more than half the people, it was recognised
to be the relic of a social order which was dead or dying. But
it was nevertheless the key to a past that looked back, beyond
the age of the peasantry, to an age of kings and heroes. Greece
and Rome had supplied a heroic past for all educated men
in the eighteenth century; the nineteenth-century nationalist
wanted a past of his own. He found it in the histories of
Sylvester O'Halloran and Geoffrey Keating, which wove the
threads of legend and history together into a heroic tapestry.
From these intimations of antiquity (and, let it be added, from
emulation of the popular success of Sir Walter Scott) there
came a spate of balladry—some good, some bad; some authentic, some fake; but all of it rendering in some way a sense of
Irishness. It can be heard in the songs of Thomas Moore, as the
elegiac note of a lament for a lost world. And you can find it—
more artless but more defiant—throughout the poems of *The
Nation* and in little green volumes published by James Duffy,
with harps and shamrocks on the covers and the Irish words
spelt out in graveyard type. Much of it is sorry stuff, no better
than romantic bombast, and its vision of nobility is aristocratic
and militaristic:

> O for a steed, a rushing steed, when Briain smote down the
> Dane,
> Or a place beside great Aodh O'Neill, when Bagenal the
> bold was slain.

But through the translations of Mangan and Ferguson plain
people did get a glimpse, as through stained glass, of their own
past; and in the songs of *The Nation* they found a simple ideal
of a noble, gallant, spirited Irish race.

This notion of a *race*, distinct from other races, runs through
the writing of the mid-century. Even Davis, for all his pluralist
philosophy, is full of it. It met English jingoism with Irish
jingoism; it met *Punch*'s caricatures of the Paddy with its own
travesties:

Where an Irish peasant is gay and gallant, an English boor is sullen and sensual. The Saxon plots a vice where the Celt meditates a gallantry; and when he falls into habitual immorality he wallows like a hog in the stye of his moral filth, till he becomes the very beast he resembles. . . . The gay, bold, joyous Irishman has no tendency to the darker vices. His animal spirits and his love of fun supply him with abundant materials for enjoyment.[4]

The anthropology belongs strictly to the school of Dion Boucicault; but the writer is making the distinction that matters. The Irish race must be distinguished above all from the *English* race; and one of the best ways to point up the distinction is to use emotive words like Celt and Saxon. Neither word has, in the context, any discernible meaning at all. They exist to make a noise : the one a noble noise, and the other a derogatory noise. The noises are still audible, off-stage, when we come to the movement of the Gaelic revival.

* * *

The Gaelic League was founded with the purpose of defining the Irish identity by the study and revival of the Irish language. Douglas Hyde, its first president, was a Protestant and a scholar —a scholar who did not view the language as a field of antiquarian study alone, but was deeply involved with its living tradition. He associated the language expressly with the need for 'a de-anglicisation of Ireland'.

Just when we should be starting to build up anew the Irish race and the Gaelic nation—as within our own recollection Greece has been built up anew—we find ourselves despoiled of the bricks of nationality.[5]

The task of the Gaelic League was to make the bricks.

It is impossible to read about the early days of the Gaelic League without catching some spark of that enthusiasm which, for a time, brought together men and women of all backgrounds, giving them a common ideal and a common purpose. George A. Birmingham, who was one of them, has likened it to the primitive church :

Its members were conscious of having discovered a source of

light, a way of joy. They were eagerly desirous of sharing their treasure with others.[6]

T. W. Rolleston saw the league as 'the last effort of our Irish spirit for nationality, and a personal independence'.[7] Horace Plunkett thought the league had discovered the difference between nationality and nationalism. The movement, he thought, was not necessarily separatist: 'There has never been any essential opposition between the English connection and Irish nationality.'[8]

Like Plunkett, most of the Anglo-Irish who supported the movement probably did so without any very clear idea of what 'de-anglicisation' might imply. Rolleston grouped the league with organisations like the Feis Ceoil, the Irish Literary Theatre and the Irish Arts and Crafts Society: 'These movements are one and all founded on a non-political basis, and one and all have set their doors wide to Home Ruler and Unionist alike.'[9] In some ways its opponents had a clearer understanding of what it was all about. Mahaffy of Trinity, the arch-conservative —Oscar Wilde's mentor, and eventually Provost—thought the league was setting up 'a false test of nationality instead of a true one': it was 'a profound mistake that distinct nationality is only to be sustained by distinct language'. Opponents of the movement were not to be tolerated:

> If any one of them speaks out his mind, the whole posse sets upon him; he is denounced as unpatriotic, dishonest, as a disguised enemy, from every point of view no Irishman. And yet he may have declared himself owing to an earnest desire to do his country good.[10]

Mahaffy, of course, knew nothing about Irish, and he despised what he did not know: 'a most difficult and useless language— not only useless, but a mischievous obstacle to civilisation.'[11] In his own terms, he was right. What he meant by civilisation was almost exactly the same as what Hyde meant by anglicisation. W. P. Ryan expressed the confrontation in a single sentence: 'We are working for a new Irish civilisation, quite distinct from the English.'[12]

Gaelic society had been shattered before 1700. The new civilisation would have to be built, presumably, from the fragments that survived in the peasant cottages of the south and west. It would have to stand without the intellectual framework which had been common to European culture for the past two centuries. It would have to root itself in a distant and legendary past. It would have to ignore, if not to obliterate, all the close commerce of generations between two neighbouring peoples. It would have to express itself in a language unknown to a majority of the nation, and to almost all the educated classes. Under the very noses of the people who were setting out to define Irish culture, that culture itself was changing. In the fifty years since the death of Davis the railway had linked up the four corners of Ireland, and the steamship had put a bridge across the Irish Sea. O'Connell had had to set out for parliament in a stage-coach; Parnell could get into a first-class carriage at eight o'clock in the evening and be in London by morning; and the telegraph would bring back the report of his speech in the House in time to be printed in the Irish newspapers next day. The cultural union had in fact been much more real than the legislative union. It is impossible to escape a sense of wonderland when one read the journalists of Irish Ireland apologising in English (which they wrote very well) for using the language of the foreigner, because, unhappily, most of their readers did not understand their native tongue.

Access to the new civilisation depended on a key, which was the language. The right to have the key depended on something else, and this they called race. In Griffith's paper, the *United Irishman*, the note of racial distinction is struck again and again. One must not exaggerate : this was the idiom of the period; and Griffith had not lived to see Hitler. Nevertheless, the note of Gaelic racial exclusivism, heard at this time, inevitably set the Irish Irelanders at a distance from those of the so-called Anglo-Irish who valued the 'Anglo' part of their heritage. But Griffith was driving all the time towards the logic of a political definition. The going was about to become sticky for well-meaning loyalists like Capt. the Hon. Otway Cuffe, president of the Gaelic League in Kilkenny, who 'did not believe that an Irish Ireland was incompatible with loyalty to the King'.[13] The job of Sinn Féin was to make it incompatible; and Sinn Féin succeeded. In 1915 the Gaelic League was captured by the political revolutionaries, and Hyde gave up the presidency. The coup, writes an authority on the period, 'put an end to his dream of making the Irish language a common bond between Irishmen of differing allegiances and made it seem the property of one section only. This he regretted profoundly.'[14]

* * *

'Nationalism is a communal thing. No community, no nationalism.' Thus, in his most magisterial tones, Daniel Corkery quashed an adversary who tried to make the case that Swift and other Anglo-Irishmen of the eighteenth century represented 'Protestant nationalism'.

> Nationalism is tangible only in its communal pieties. The origin of them, the growth of them, the reverence for them, the homogeneity of them, are the considerations we should keep before our minds. Protestant nationalism will not stand against such tests.[15]

Corkery's matrix of nationalism was a Gaelic Ireland, rural in ethos and Catholic in faith. It does not readily admit anyone of an urban tradition; it does not readily admit any Protestant. The bulk of writing by Irishmen in English he refuses to classify even as Anglo-Irish : it is moulded by alien influences, it is addressed to an alien audience, it is written largely by expatriates. 'This word', he adds in a revealing footnote, 'must serve, although of course it is not the right word to apply to such writers as, for instance, Swift, Goldsmith, Shaw—writers for whom Ireland was never a *patria* in any sense.'[16] Synge, by being absorbed into nationalism, acquired a *patria*; and *Riders to the Sea* is 'the unique example where an Ascendancy writer entered with any effective intimacy into the life of the Catholic Gaelic people'.[17]

This is exclusivism at its most stringent. It appears to leave most Protestant Irishmen with no fatherland at all. By this test, not many members of the minority will qualify for the nation, not even the nation's greatest leaders, thinkers, poets. Charles Stewart Parnell, who waged and nearly won the war of attrition at Westminster; William Butler Yeats, whose verse forms a counterpoint to Irish thought throughout this period of self-discovery : they are members of the wrong tribe, and they cannot be admitted to the nation, unless the nation is big enough to embrace all its tribes.

* * *

If the linguistic heritage of Ireland belongs to the Catholics, then the physical heritage belongs, in a very great degree, to the Protestants. There are, of course, ample historical reasons. The Reformation delivered most of the Christian monuments into the hands of the Established Church, so that almost every ancient ecclesiastical building in the country is the property of the Church of Ireland. To find a High Cross you look in a Protestant graveyard. The great houses of the countryside—such of them as survive—date from the period of the Ascendancy, when only the grandees of the Establishment were in a position to build mansions and lay out estates. The Georgian squares of Dublin and the finest of its public buildings—these too are part of the legacy of the Ascendancy. Protestants laid out most of the notable gardens of Ireland, and in many cases still maintain them. All this they did, no doubt, because they were the class with power, the class with privilege, the class with wealth. Yet they had, and perhaps still have, a special feeling for the country. Arthur Synan put his finger on it sixty years ago :

> In one point of patriotism Protestants commonly excel Catholics; they have an intense devotion to the soil of Ireland as a physical thing. They have a real love for its beauty. They delight in the amenities of Irish life. The idea that Ireland is a place or state of punishment, where some stay for a time, is much less common among Protestants than among Catholics. They seem to love the country in a material sense, as distinguished from the people.[18]

Protestants have no doubt been insensitive to the spiritual environment represented by the Irish language. But the zealots of the revival, on the other hand, have been so single-minded in their concern for the language that they have been careless—or even resentful—of the physical environment created under the Protestant hegemony. Both elements, taken together, make up the heritage of the nation.

* * *

The time has come, I think, to take a new look at the terms in which we define nationality; and it would be no harm to begin by looking around us. The people we see are English-speaking people; they read the *Sunday Express*, they watch

BBC television; they govern themselves in a parliamentary style
that recognisably derives from Westminster. There are weekend
excursions from Dublin for football matches in Liverpool and
Manchester. Upwards of a million Irish people live and work
in Britain; they vote in British elections and even stand for the
United Kingdom parliament; they come home in their thousands
for the Christmas holidays, and bring their mothers presents
from Marks and Spencers.

If culture is the pattern in which we live our lives, then
Irish culture has been interpenetrated—over centuries, over
generations, but with ever-increasing intensity in recent decades
—by the culture of the neighbouring island. And that culture
itself, of course, is an amalgam of elements that are native,
elements that are European, elements that are transatlantic. The
Gaelic element in Irish culture is of special importance because
it is distinctive. But if we are moulded by our past, then we
are moulded by the whole of our past. We can no more select
the strains that are to influence our culture than we can choose
the genes that make up our physical organism.

But there is, all the same, an Irish nationality, quite distinct
from the English. You can almost smell it in the air at Dublin
Bay. Catholics and Protestants, Murphys and Barbers, are all
aware of it : you have only to see them gravitate together under
a foreign sky. The culture that they share is the culture of a
small community, still strongly rooted in the family group, still
closely associated with the countryside; it is the culture of a
society in which religion still forms part of the predominant
pattern. Their nationality is best defined, perhaps, in terms of a
system of communication. They respond to the same signals,
they exchange the same idioms, they speak—in the very broadest
sense—the same language.

Once we recognise the living reality of this national identity,
we are liberated from the prickly defensiveness which obliges
us to insist on the primacy of one element over another. And
we can begin, gradually perhaps, to understand that this
national identity extends to all the provinces, north and south
of the border. In a recent paper on cultural traditions Liam de
Paor argues that

The element of shared experience is enormous; but in the

South we have liked to forget about the British parts of our inheritance; in the North we have tried to forget about the Irish parts. Saving the important matter of religion—and this is, of course, a major part of anyone's culture—the cultural traditions of by far the greater part of the present population of this island are not all that different. It is the myths that have differed, and these no longer serve the health of either of our societies. . . . In this whole matter of *identity*, we should, rather than try to bully one another into accepting the Britishness of Ulster or the Irishness of Ireland, endorse the principle of individual liberty, which is nowhere more important than here, and offer to everyone who lives on this island his free choice.[19]

Charles Stewart Parnell, gentleman, landowner, Protestant and Irish patriot, said it in simpler words :

We cannot give up a single Irishman.

Sources and Acknowledgments

Among the many books which I have consulted in the course of my research a handful have been of outstanding importance. They are:

F. S. L. Lyons, *Ireland Since the Famine*, London 1971: a masterly survey of modern Irish history from 1850 to 1969.

J. C. Beckett, *The Making of Modern Ireland, 1603–1923*, London 1966: a very well balanced one-volume work by a Northern historian—especially useful for the earlier period.

J. H. Whyte, *Church and State in Modern Ireland, 1923–70*, Dublin 1971: the one indispensable work on church-state relations, Dr Whyte's book carries the main theme to which the story of the Protestant minority is, as it were, the descant.

Patrick Buckland, *Irish Unionism* 1: *The Anglo-Irish and the New Ireland, 1885–1922*, Dublin and New York 1972: the most up-to-date study of Unionism as a political organisation.

D. H. Akenson, *The Church of Ireland: Ecclesiastical Reform and Revolution, 1800–85*, New Haven and London 1971. Also by the same author, *The Irish Education Experiment*, London and Toronto 1970. Two detailed but readable studies on related aspects of the nineteenth century.

For more specialised reading, W. Alison Phillips, ed., *History of the Church of Ireland*, 3 vols, Oxford 1933–34, is the standard work on Irish Anglicanism and is indispensable in any study of the subject. To some extent it supersedes R. Mant, *History of the Church of Ireland*, 2 vols, London 1840, though the latter is still useful. The basic work on Presbyterianism is J. S. Reid, *History of the Presbyterian Church in Ireland*, 3 vols, Belfast 1867; it is supplemented by J. M. Barkley, *Short History of the Presbyterian Church in Ireland*, Belfast 1959. J. C. Beckett, *Protestant Dissent in Ireland, 1687–1780,* London 1943, contains an excellent modern survey of Presbyterianism and concise accounts of the minor denominations.

The various series of Thomas Davis Lectures, commissioned for broadcasting by Radio Telefís Éireann and subsequently published, have done very much to bridge the gap between the scholar and the layman, and have aided my understanding of many aspects of my subject. Finally I must mention how much the past has been illuminated for me by works of fiction, notably by the novels of George A. Birmingham (Canon J. O. Hannay).

For library services I am indebted to the National Library of Ireland, Trinity College, the Representative Body of the Church of Ireland, and the Royal Dublin Society. The lending facilities offered by the last-named have been of special importance to a part-time researcher who could not always accommodate himself to the hours of reading-rooms. I should like to take this opportunity to express my particular gratitude to the former Librarian of the RDS, Mr Desmond Clarke, for his personal interest and advice. Mr Malcolm Macourt, of the University of Durham, has kindly devoted his time to checking my statistics. Among others whom I must thank for their interest and assistance are Dr Edward MacLysaght, formerly of the Irish Manuscripts Commission; Dr F. S. L. Lyons, of Trinity College, Dublin; Mr Liam de Paor, of University College, Dublin; the Rev. T. P. MacInerney, OP, and Mrs Catherine McGuinness.

In attempting to interpret a living community—however diminished—I have of course depended above all on the people of that community. I have travelled to at least fifteen of the Republic's twenty-six counties and I have talked to Protestants of all age-groups, both laymen and clerics. Such help cannot be acknowledged specifically. I hope that those who gave it so freely will accept this general acknowledgment: my contact with them has not only provided information about the present day, but has formed the spectrum of opinion through which I have come to view the past.

Finally I should like to express my thanks to Radio Telefís Éireann, and in particular to Mr T. P. Hardiman, Director General, and Mr Michael Garvey, Controller of Programmes, who have been uniformly helpful and encouraging to me in this diversion from the serious business of broadcasting.

J.W., January 1975.

Notes

INTRODUCTION (pp 1–7)

1. Arthur Synan, 'Our Protestant Brother', *New Ireland Review* (Dec. 1908).
2. 'A Graduate of the University of Pennsylvania' [Matthew Woods], *Rambles of a Physician*, (privately published) Philadelphia 1889.
3. Lennox Robinson, *A Young Man from the South*, Dublin 1917, 39.
4. George A. Birmingham, *An Irishman Looks at his World*, London 1919, 119.

CHAPTER 1 (pp 9–16)

1. R. B. McDowell, 'Dublin and Belfast: A Comparison' in *Social Life in Ireland 1800–45* (Thomas Davis Lectures), Dublin 1957, 18.
2. Brendan M. Walsh, *Religion and Demographic Behaviour in Ireland* (Economic and Social Research Institute Paper No. 55), Dublin 1970.
3. Howard Robinson, 'A Study of the Church of Ireland Population of Ardfert, Co. Kerry, 1971', *Economic and Social Review* (Dublin, Oct. 1972).

CHAPTER 2 (pp 17–30)

1. Anon., *Forty Years in the Church of Ireland; or, The Pastor, the Parish and the People, 1840–80*, London n.d.

CHAPTER 3 (pp 31–40)

1. George Bernard Shaw, *John Bull's Other Island* (preface), London 1909, viii.
2. Edmund Spenser, *A View of the Present State of Ireland* (London 1633), ed. W. L. Renwick, Oxford 1970, 161.
3. E. A. D'Alton, *History of Ireland*, Dublin n.d., III, 25.

4. J. C. Beckett, *The Making of Modern Ireland, 1603–1923*, London 1966, 39.

5. John Wesley, *Journals*, London n.d., II, 68.

6. Arthur Young, *Tours in Ireland*, London 1780, II, 57.

7. Wesley, *Journals*, II, 68.

8. James Frost, *History and Topography of the Co. Clare*, Dublin 1893, 630.

9. Young, *Tours in Ireland*, I, 378.

10. *Ibid.*, II, 29. 11. *Ibid.*, II, 30.

12. Arland Ussher, *The Face and Mind of Ireland*, London 1949, 129.

13. Quoted in Daniel Corkery, *The Hidden Ireland*, Dublin 1941, 218.

14. Edward MacLysaght, *Irish Families*, Dublin 1957, 187; *More Irish Families*, Dublin 1960; *Supplement to Irish Families*, Dublin 1964. (Also conversation with the author.)

CHAPTER 4 (pp 41–52)

1. Theobald Wolfe Tone, *Autobiography*. Quoted in *The Best of Tone*, ed. P. Mac Aonghusa and L. Ó. Reagáin, Cork 1972, 106–7.

2. W. T. Latimer, *History of Presbyterianism in Ireland*, Belfast 1908, 391, 395.

3. W. Marrable, *Rise and Progress of the Irish Church Missions*, Dublin 1850, 4.

4. Élie Halévy, *History of the English People in the Nineteenth Century*, London 1951, IV, 347.

5. William Rooney, *Prose Writings*, Dublin and Waterford 1909, 7.

6. D. Bowen, *Souperism—Myth or Reality?*, Cork 1970, 119.

7. Marrable, *Irish Church Missions*, 23.

8. J. Garrett, *Good News from Ireland*, London 1863, 18.

9. Anon., *Forty Years in the Church of Ireland*.

10. E. R. Norman, *The Catholic Church and Irish Politics in the 1860s* (Dublin Historical Association), Dundalk 1969, 16–17.

11. H. Kingsmill Moore, *Reminiscences and Reflections from Some Sixty Years of Life in Ireland*, London 1930, 183.

CHAPTER 5 (pp 53–69)

1. George Bernard Shaw, *Sixteen Self-Sketches*, London 1949, 46. (Reprinted from *M.A.P.*, Sep. 1898.)

2. *Irish Times*, 22 Jun. 1897.

3. *Daily Express* (Dublin), 22 Jun. 1897.

4. Sean O'Casey, *I Knock at the Door*, London 1939.

5. *Irish Society*, 8 Feb. 1888.   6. *Ibid.*

7. Shaw, *Sixteen Self-Sketches*, 46.

8. L. A. G. Strong, *The Garden*, London 1939, 161.

9. G. B. Shaw, note on a MS. by Charles Shaw (National Library of Ireland).

10. Arthur E. Clery, 'The Religious Angle in Irish Life', *Studies* (Sep. 1915).

11. Wilmot Irwin, *Betrayal in Ireland*, Belfast n.d., 7.

12. George A. Birmingham, *Hyacinth*, London 1906, 26.

13. F. S. L. Lyons, *Ireland Since the Famine*, London 1971, 20.

14. E. Œ. Somerville and Martin Ross, *The Real Charlotte*, London 1896.

15. Edward Lysaght, *The Gael*, Dublin 1919, 65.

16. R. Lucas, *Colonel Saunderson, M.P., A Memoir*, London 1908, 113.

17. Irish Loyal and Patriotic Union, *The Real Dangers of Home Rule*, Dublin 1886.

18. Horace Plunkett, *Ireland in the New Century*, London 1905, 64.

19. Ian D'Alton, 'Southern Irish Unionism: A Study of Cork Unionists, 1884–1914', *Transactions of the Royal Historical Society*, 5th series, XXXIII (1973).

20. Quoted in Patrick Buckland, *Irish Unionism* 1 : *The Anglo-Irish and the New Ireland, 1885–1922*, Dublin and New York 1972, 18.

21. *New Ireland Review*, Feb. 1908.

22. P. Finlay, 'Religion and Civil Life', *New Ireland Review*, Feb. 1901.

23. House of Commons reports, 13 Jun. 1912 (quoted by F. E. Smith).

24. O'Casey, *I Knock at the Door*, 27.

25. Margaret Digby, *Horace Plunkett, an Anglo-American Irishman*, Oxford 1949, 93.

26. C. H. Rolleston, *Portrait of an Irishman: A Biographical Sketch of T. W. Rolleston*, London 1939, 118.

27. Quoted by Brian Inglis, *Roger Casement*, London 1973, 387.

28. House of Commons reports, 12 Jun. 1912.

29. *Irish Times*, 23 Jun. 1897.

30. Rolleston, *Portrait of an Irishman*, 60.

31. Digby, *Horace Plunkett*, 293.

32. C. Cruise O'Brien, Introduction to *The Shaping of Modern Ireland* (Thomas Davis Lectures), London 1960, 5.

33. Edward Lysaght, *A Memoir of Sir Horace Plunkett*, Dublin 1916, 24.

34. Horace Plunkett, *A Better Way*, Dublin 1914, 21.

CHAPTER 6 (pp 70–9)

1. *Irish Times*, 30 Sep. 1912.
2. House of Commons reports, 13 Jun. 1912.
3. *Irish Times*, 18 Jul. 1914.
4. House of Commons reports, 3 Aug. 1914.
5. *Ibid.*, 15 Sep. 1914. 6. *Irish Times*, 4 Aug. 1914.
7. Lord Dunraven, *Past Times and Pastimes*, London 1922, 52.
8. Quoted in Lennox Robinson, *Bryan Cooper, A Memoir*, London 1931, 88.
9. Robert Kee, *The Green Flag*, London 1972, 525, 594. (From *Freeman's Journal*, 16 and 19 Oct. 1915; *Irish Independent*, 11 Nov. 1916.)
10. Buckland, *Irish Unionism* 1, 39.
11. George Seaver, *John Allen Fitzgerald Gregg, Archbishop*, London and Dublin 1963, 92.
12. W. Alison Phillips, *The Revolution in Ireland, 1906–23*, London 1923, 105.
13. G. B. Shaw, 'Neglected Morals of the Easter Rising', *New Statesman*, 6 May 1916.
14. *Freeman's Journal*, 5 May 1916 (special edition covering 26–29 Apr. and 1–5 May).
15. Phillips, *The Revolution in Ireland*, 106.
16. *Irish Times*, 21 Nov. 1921.

CHAPTER 7 (pp 80–90)

1. Ernest Blythe, in conversation with the author, 1973.
2. Tom Barry, *Guerrilla Days in Ireland*, Dublin 1949, 4.
3. Lionel Fleming, *Head or Harp?*, London 1965, 63.
4. Lady Gregory, *Journals*, ed. Lennox Robinson, London 1946, 13.
5. Barry, *Guerrilla Days in Ireland*, 95.
6. Quoted in Lennox Robinson, *Bryan Cooper*.
7. Frank Gallagher, *The Anglo-Irish Treaty*, ed. T. P. O'Neill, Dublin 1965, 43.
8. Earl of Midleton, *Records and Reactions, 1856–1939*, London 1939, 264.
9. Phillips, *The Revolution in Ireland*, 280 n.
10. *The Times*, 8 Dec. 1921. 11. *Irish Times*, 16 Jan. 1922.
12. *Ibid.*, 13 May 1922. 13. *Ibid.*, 16 Jun. 1922.

CHAPTER 8 (pp 91–102)

1. Dáil reports, 6 Jan. 1922.
2. James G. Douglas, papers in possession of Mr J. H. Douglas.
3. W. B. Stanford, *A Recognised Church*, Dublin 1944, 16.
4. Seaver, *J. A. F. Gregg*, 126. 5. *Ibid.*, 116.
6. Robinson, *Bryan Cooper*, 147.
7. Fleming, *Head or Harp?*, 93.
8. Seanad reports, 14 Nov. 1923.
9. Dáil reports, 19 Dec. 1921.
10. *Irish Times*, 7 Dec. 1921.
11. Dáil reports, 17 Jun. 1931.

CHAPTER 9 (pp 103–11)

1. *Irish Times*, 13 Feb. 1932.
2. Seaver, *J. A. F. Gregg*, 190.
3. *Church of Ireland Gazette*, 22 Jan. 1937.
4. *Ibid.*, 15 Jan. 1937.
5. Dáil reports, 11 Dec. 1936.
6. *Irish Times*, 11 Dec. 1936.
7. Edward Lysaght, *The Gael*, 256.
8. *Irish Times*, 27 Sep. 1912.
9. Brian Inglis, *West Briton*, London 1962, 53.
10. V. H. S. Mercier, 'The Times (Irish)', *The Bell* (Jan. 1945).
11. *Irish Times*, 5 Jun. 1937.
12. *Church of Ireland Gazette*, 15 Jan. 1937.
13. The Earl of Longford and T. P. O'Neill, *Eamon de Valera*, London 1970, 354.
14. For a full account of this important incident, see J. H. Whyte, *Church and State in Modern Ireland*.

CHAPTER 10 (pp 112–28)

1. W. Philbin, Bishop of Clonfert, 'A City on a Hill', *Studies* (Autumn 1957).
2. Whyte, *Church and State in Modern Ireland*, 48.
3. C. Cruise O'Brien, *States of Ireland*, London 1972, 121.
4. Quoted in Whyte, *Church and State in Modern Ireland*, 158.
5. For a full account of the censorship up to 1968, see M. Adams, *Censorship—the Irish Experience*, Dublin 1968.
6. Seanad reports, 11 Jun. 1925.
7. *Bunreacht na hEireann*, 1937.
8. *Irish Times*, 12 Dec. 1945.
9. Presbyterian Synod of Dublin, *Church and State Report 1973* (privately circulated). The report contains a full critique of the constitution from the Presbyterian viewpoint.

10. Dáil reports, 1 Aug. 1934.
11. Paul Blanshard, *The Irish and Catholic Power*, Boston 1953, 157.
12. *Irish Times*, 26 Nov. 1973.
13. *Irish Times*, 20 Dec. 1973.
14. *Bunreacht na hEireann*, 1937.
15. Dáil reports, 4 Jun. 1937.
16. *Irish Law Times Reports* (Cook v. Carroll), LXXIX, 1945.
17. *Ibid.* (Tilson v. Tilson), LXXXVI, 1952.
18. *Irish Times*, 31 Jul. 1952.

CHAPTER 11 (pp 129–36)
1. *Irish Times*, 27 Sep. 1973.
2. *Motu Proprio: Apostolic Letter determining Norms for Mixed Marriages*, Vatican 1970.
3. *Irish Times*, 6 Sep. 1974. 4. *Ibid.*, 7 Sep. 1974.

CHAPTER 12 (pp 137–57)
1. Donald H. Akenson, *The Irish Education Experiment*, London and Toronto 1970, 390.
2. *Ibid.* 3. *Ibid.*
4. Horace Plunkett, *Ireland in the New Century*, 152.
5. *Catholic Bulletin*, Jan. 1927.
6. *The Times*, 4 Dec. 1926.
7. Background information from an unpublished paper by Micheál Johnston.
8. *Catholic Bulletin*, Jan. 1927. 9. Synod Papers, 1965.
10. *Ibid.*, 1973.
11. George A. Birmingham, *An Irishman Looks at his World*, London 1919, 152.

CHAPTER 13 (pp 158–69)
1. M. Johnston, unpublished paper.
2. L. Paul-Dubois, *Contemporary Ireland*, Dublin 1911, 193.
3. *Ibid.*, 189. 4. *Irish Times*, 2 Jun. 1902.
5. Arthur E. Clery, 'The Religious Angle in Irish Life', *Studies* (Sep. 1915).
6. *Irish Times*, 31 Jul. 1973.
7. *Hibernia*, 2 Mar. 1973.
8. *Irish Times*, 16 Apr. 1949; 15–25 Nov. 1950; 1 Mar. 1951.
9. Dáil reports, 17 Jun. 1931.

10. Seaver, *J. A. F. Gregg*, 334.

11. T. de Vere White, 'Freemasons' in *Secret Societies in Ireland*, ed. T. D. Williams, Dublin and New York 1973, 50.

12. Rev. R. J. Kerr, contributing to a symposium in *The Bell* (Jun. 1944).

CHAPTER 14 (pp 170–82)

1. F. D. How, *William Conyngham Plunket, A Memoir*, London 1900, 78.

2. R. P. C. Hanson, Bishop of Clogher, address delivered at Virginia, Co. Cavan, 1 Oct. 1972. (From MS.)

3. J. P. Mahaffy, 'The Romanisation of Ireland', *Nineteenth Century* (Jul. 1901).

4. *Irish Times*, 17 May 1974.

5. Seaver, *J. A. F. Gregg*, 141–58.

6. H. R. McAdoo, Bishop of Ossory, in conversation with the author.

7. Westminster Confession of Faith, Edinburgh and London 1913, 39.

8. M. Woods, *Rambles of a Physician*,

9. Olive G. Goodbody, Introduction to *Guide to Irish Quaker Records, 1654–1860*, Dublin 1967.

CHAPTER 15 (pp 183–93)

1. Arthur Griffith, ed., *Thomas Davis: The Thinker and Teacher*, Dublin 1914, 12.

2. Daniel Corkery: 'The Nation That Was Never a Nation', *Studies* (Dec. 1934).

3. *The Bell*, Jun. 1944.

4. *The Voice of the Nation*, Dublin 1844.

5. Quoted in Myles Dillon, 'Douglas Hyde' in *The Shaping of Modern Ireland*, London 1960, 54.

6. George A. Birmingham, *An Irishman Looks at his World*, 160.

7. Rolleston : *Portrait of an Irish Gentleman*, 52.

8. *Ibid.*   9. *Ibid.*, 60.

10. J. P. Mahaffy, 'The Modern Babel', *Nineteenth Century* (Nov. 1896).

11. *Ibid.*   12. *United Irishman*, 8 Feb. 1902.

13. *Ibid.*, 26 May 1902.

14. Seán Ó Luing, 'Douglas Hyde and the Gaelic League', *Studies* (Summer 1973).

15. Corkery in *Studies* (Dec. 1934).

16. Corkery, *Synge and Anglo-Irish Literature*, Cork 1947, 3 n.

17. *Ibid.*, 109.

18. A. Synan, 'Our Protestant Brother', *New Ireland Review* (Dec. 1908).

19. Liam de Paor, 'Cultural Traditions'. (Address delivered to the Irish Association, Dublin, 23 Feb. 1973.)

Index